CHASING GREATNESS

CHASING

The Young Professional's Guide to a Dynamic Life

GREATNESS

Towan Isom

FOREWORD BY **Valorie Burton**

MAVERICK MEDIA™

MAVERICK MEDIA™
1433 Duncan Street NE
Washington DC 20002
www.isommediallc.com

Distributed in United States, Canada, and in the United Kingdom by Ingram.

Cover and text design by theBookDesigners

Library of Congress Cataloging-in-Publication Data

Includes bibliographical references and index
ISBN-13: 978-0-9815834-0-2
ISBN-10: 0-9815834-0-7

Printed in the United States of America.
First printing, 2009

1 2 3 4 5 6 7 8 9 10/13 12 11 10 09

In reaffirming the greatness of our nation we understand that greatness is never a given. It must be earned. Our journey has never been one of short-cuts or settling for less. It has not been the path for the faint-hearted, for those that prefer leisure over work, or seek only the pleasures of riches and fame. Rather, it has been the risk-takers, the doers, the makers of things—some celebrated, but more often men and women obscure in their labor—who have carried us up the long rugged path towards prosperity and freedom.

—President Barack Obama, 2009 Inauguration Address

Contents

Foreword

Nothing is more useful a gift in bringing a vision to life than passion. I first met Towan Isom when I spoke at her spectacular Spiritually Speaking Tea & Talk in Washington, D.C., in 2005. What first struck me about her was her sincerity and transparency. Then I noticed the way she sets a big vision – and achieves it. In the years that I have known Towan, her passion for bringing women together and helping women live fully and freely is perhaps her most powerful asset.

Over the years, we've worked on several projects together. With each one, her special touch – a mix of elegance, excellence, and faith – makes all the difference. She's produced several events in which I was the featured speaker. When it was time to revamp my marketing efforts, Towan led the way! From photo shoots to video shoots to my website, Towan's special touch has been an integral part of my business. And now you are about to experience that for yourself!

What Towan shares on these pages is a heartfelt desire for you to live the life you are called to live. Her words are rooted in her faith in Jesus Christ, and all that He stands for. One of the main things I love about *Chasing Greatness* is that it is not just a book to read, but a workbook to complete. Towan offers questions with spaces for answers, checklists, and even opportunities to interview others. Completing these exercises will help anyone in the pursuit of greatness. This is a valuable tool that I can read again and again to monitor my progression to greatness.

The abundant life overflows with Jesus' love, grace, and mercy. If you are ready to embrace that abundance, read on and let the journey begin.

Warm wishes,
Valorie Burton

Acknowledgments

I would like to thank my mother, Theretha, for being my super cheer-leader; my brother, Tyrone, for teaching me patience; and my friends, by whom I measure my progress. I'd like to thank my editor for helping me through the tedious but invaluable editing process.

I thank my faults for keeping me humble, my successes for keeping me interested, my future children for keeping me purposed, and Spiritually Speaking supporters for trusting me with their spiritual edification.

Most importantly, I thank Jesus Christ who is the substance of my existence and the measuring rod for my capacity.

Introduction

Greatness can be grasped! When we move forward in expectation, we move toward what *will be*, not what *could be*. It is in that confidence that we are able to grasp our greatness.

A few years ago I had the opportunity to meet John C. Maxwell at a leadership summit. Maxwell, a world-renowned speaker, lecturer, and former pastor, has written more than 20 books on leadership. During Maxwell's speech, he was asked how he knew so much about leadership. Maxwell responded, "It's in the Bible." The attendee said, "What?" Not because he didn't hear Maxwell, but because he was surprised by the answer. Maxwell repeated, "It's in the Bible."

I tell that story because the wisdom in this book is a culmination of years of my professional experience at one of Viacom's biggest cash cows, starting and successfully running my own consulting firm for over ten years, and growing an online community to over 8,000 subscribers, and my understanding of the Bible.

There are many things that undermine our greatness, including doubt. Doubt debilitates our anticipation. **However, removing doubt and applying the tools in this book will enable you to claim and possess the place you are destined to occupy—greatness!**

As we evolve, our ability to produce successfully is directly enhanced by our inner ability to visualize the outcome. Speculation is for us, but certainty is for God. Certainty brings confidence that doubt doesn't. It's only with the certainty mindset that we can claim and possess our greatness. Certainty is gained through growing closer to God, applying biblical truths, self-discovery, and applying the principles in *Chasing Greatness*. The chapters in this book offer practical steps for our professional and personal lives. Use them!

It's no coincidence that we are at a time of transition in our world and in our lives. Our lives are less about *if* we transition, but more about *when* and *how* we transition. Although targeted to young professionals, *Chasing Greatness* has something for all adults with a desire to move from ordinary lives to extraordinary greatness. This book is for those *worthy* of greatness and willing to *work* for it.

It's in the *push* or *chase* for greatness that we discover who we really are. Here's to greatness; now go *chase it!*

What Is Greatness?

CHAPTER 1
What Is Greatness?

Many people equate greatness with wealth and material possessions. It is only after you get the stuff and max out your credit cards that you discover how unhappy, unfulfilled, and unsatisfied you are with life.

Greatness goes beyond money; it supersedes material things like cars, houses, and jewelry. Various dictionaries use these synonyms for "great": extensive, outstanding, powerful, influential, skillful, and significant—nothing to do with money. I define greatness as, "the collision of character and service."

In my early 20s I worked at Black Entertainment Television (BET). I thought, *This is the life!* I was young, smart, and attractive, a triple threat for the entertainment and television industry. My only goal was to make it from Washington, D.C., to the Big Apple, New York City, and to take it by storm. Hurricane Towan was going to bring thunder to the city that never sleeps, and I had a three-year plan to make it happen. Five years and three mortgages later, I was still in D.C. By then I had accumulated my share of celebrity stories, gossip, and memorable experiences about the lengths to which people will go to just to be in the same room as an A-list actor or playoff athlete with Super Bowl potential. I wouldn't believe the sights or stories I observed during my BET stint if I hadn't experienced them first-hand.

It wasn't until the summer of year six, while at an industry party, that I realized something was missing. Conversations with some celebs and groupies centered more on superficial traits and their trysts than on internal qualities and character. Thriving and seemingly upwardly-mobile people who looked successful externally were empty inside, and they were yearning for significance through the industry. The influence we give other people over our lives when we don't have our own sense of significance is amazing.

At BET, I worked with numerous artists, celebrities, and producers for many years. Looking back, it is interesting to see how humble the celebrities were in the beginning, citing their troubled childhoods and their difficult upbringings. Initially, artists only wanted to make great music; yet after a few successes, some just wanted to make millions. What happened to the art, the message...the substance? I remember being at that industry party thinking, *This is it...this is the industry...and we are the generation that's going to do it differently.* Now, years later, I have doubts. I'm not angry with anyone who wants to get paid, but getting paid and being great are two completely different things. Acquiring money is temporary. Greatness is long-term. Greatness lives beyond *you* and continues to influence *others.*

A friend once told me there are three types of people: people who make things happen, people who wait for something to happen, and people who say, "What happened?" **We each take an active role in our destiny, whether intentional or not. We can be intentional, unintentional, or inactive. Inactivity brings a culmination of circumstances and situations that may carry us to places we *don't want* to be—life happening to us and not us happening to life.** Imagine if we were intentional with our efforts and energy. Imagine if we made decisions toward *destiny* and not toward *distractions*…decisions that take us to where we *want* to be!

My hope is that this book will propel you to your intended greatness for a dynamic life by providing the tools needed to develop greatness, will disclose what keeps us from greatness, and will even show you how to create an environment that inspires others toward greatness.

What happens when there is a society of success with no soul, spirit, responsibility, or accountability? What happens when we define success by commodity and not character? What happens when we don't emulate the people we admire? *I'll tell you…we become a people of nothingness—shallow, without substance or progression.*

The greats—people like Jesus Christ, Desmond Tutu, Mother Teresa, and Dr. Martin Luther King, Jr.—paved the way for the benefits we enjoy today. Their character and contributions set them apart, but unfortunately our character doesn't always align with the people we admire. We would rather model the life of a sordid celebrity than that of the very person we say we admire. Consider: Whom do you admire, and how do you duplicate what you admire about them in your life?

The following exercises offer a greatness assessment regarding where we are and where we want to be. Below, please list the person you admire most in each of the following four areas, then explain why you admire each person. *(You do not have to know the people personally.)*

Personally_____

Name specific actions, character traits, deeds, events you admire about this person.

_____

Professionally _____

Name specific actions, character traits, deeds, events you admire about this person.

_____

Spiritually_____

Name specific actions, character traits, deeds, events you admire about this person.

_____

Politically_____

Name specific actions, character traits, deeds, events you admire about this person.

_____

The purpose of these exercises is to motivate us mentally toward greatness. Where are you in your pursuit of greatness? Let us assess using the greatness continuum. First, please check the response that applies. *On the greatness continuum, I am...*

• Walking in greatness

• En route to greatness

• Digressing from greatness

What five things make you great?

1. _____

2. _____

3. _____

4. _____

5. _____

How do you inspire others to greatness?

_____

_____

_____

Other than your family, who admires you?

_____

_____

_____

Whom have you helped? How and why did you help them? Did your help benefit you more than them?

Name: _____

How? _____ *Why?* _____

Did it benefit you or them more? Me __/Them__

Name: _____

How? _____ *Why?* _____

Did it benefit you or them more? Me __/Them__

Name: _____

How? _____ *Why?* _____

Did it benefit you or them more? Me __/Them__

Name: _____

How? _____ *Why?* _____

Did it benefit you or them more? Me __/Them__

For the remainder of this chapter, I will focus on five traits that propel us toward greatness: originality, reputation, boldness, good judgment, and prayer.

Originality

During my life I've realized that far too many of us would prefer to be a carbon copy of someone else rather than our authentic selves. Nothing is as good as the original—not the replicas on New York's Canal Street, imitation crab meat, or fat-free cheese. The original is always better.

Psalm 139:14 (KJV) says, "I will praise thee; for I am fearfully and wonderfully made: marvelous are thy works; and that my soul knoweth right well." The Hebrew word for fearfully in this passage is *yaw-daw*, which means to reverence or stand in awe. The Hebrew word for wonderfully is *paw-law*, which means to distinguish and set apart. God uniquely designed us as individuals for His purpose. If God has set us apart and reveres us, why should we want to be a clone of someone else?

We've become a society of imitators, not innovators. Imitators model someone else. Innovators create their own mold. God wants us to embrace the very thing for which we were uniquely designed, rather than try to be someone else. Biblical women, like Esther who went so boldly before King Xerxes to change the life of her people, and the prophetess Deborah, the only female judge and military leader, were innovators of their destiny. They were extraordinary because they embraced their individuality and did not remake someone else's. God is not in the business of producing carbon copies. When you have a world full of people trying to be like someone else, you have a world full of people who seldom live up to their greatness! Our purpose aligns directly with our originality. Originality can be found in our *paw-law*.

What are three things you <u>applaud</u> (are proud of) regarding yourself? *God, I celebrate the fact that I am...*

1. _____

2. _____

3. _____

What are three things you <u>wonder</u> (are curious about) regarding yourself? *God, I wonder why you made me...*

1. _____

2. _____

3. _____

What are three things you <u>esteem</u> (respect or celebrate) regarding yourself? *God, I love the fact that I have a high regard for…*

1. _____

2. _____

3. _____

Many of the core things we celebrate as we mature are the very things we possessed at age 10 before life experiences and our personal and professional compromises set in. How are you different today from the girl or boy you were at age 10?

_____

_____

_____

_____

Reputation

Your reputation is what people say about you, good or bad. In Luke 9:18-19 (NLT), Jesus asks, "Who do people say I am?"

"Well, they replied, some say John the Baptist; some say Elijah; and others say you are one of the other ancient prophets risen from the dead." Even Christ had a reputation.

In business, a good reputation is crucial. I have seen clients turn down opportunities with questionable people who could have made them tons of money. A bad reputation usually means bad business.

At BET, I had a reputation for saying what was on my mind. People knew me as a busybody with a spirited personality. I didn't see my reputation as a problem at that time. People knew if they gave me something to do, I would do it well; but if the task or project didn't make sense, I was going to question and complain. After leaving BET, I realized that what people said about me (and what some continue to say) had become my business reputation. People said I argued, complained, and always had to be right. I considered myself to be resourceful and assertive, not challenging; yet, my reality was not others' perception of me.

Your reputation is less about what you think of yourself and more about how and what you communicate to others. We exchange thoughts, feelings, and information—that is, we communicate—by writing and speaking. Thus, how I speak, when I speak, whether I speak, and even in what tone I speak are important aspects of the communication which impacts my reputation.

My immaturity says, "I don't care what others think of me." Wisdom says, "How do I communicate to others so there is less distance between my reality and others' perception of me?"

Although we cannot please everyone, we can strive to have a good reputation. Not everyone I conduct business with will like me, but all will say that I am honest, that I listen, and that I consider my words carefully before speaking. It is difficult to recover from a shaky reputation. Sure, it is possible, but it is better to prevent damaging your reputation in the first place.

I was born and lived for part of my life in Wilson, North Carolina, until my family moved to Washington, D.C., when I was nine years old. My mother found it difficult to embrace the notion of me, the quiet southern girl, now living in such a big city; she was especially concerned about my well-being. We had little money, and the places we lived were not always the best neighborhoods. My mother was continually concerned about my friends and their influence. While I was growing up, she would often say, "Birds of a feather flock together," meaning that similar people go to the same places and do the same things.

Those wise words stayed with me during high school, college, and my early career. For this reason, I learned to limit socialization with co-workers by participating in only about twenty-five percent of after-work activities and social events—just enough to stay connected and not be considered antisocial. I was pleasant, punctual, and managed to avoid office drama and casual romance. If my boss asked, I would attend. I would arrive on time and leave ten minutes after my boss did. I gave a valid and polite reason to others, such as, "It's getting late, and I have to get up early. See you guys tomorrow." Likewise, I avoided workplace gossipers. *Avoid gossipers at all cost.* When you see them, run. If you are the gossiper, stop!

Another thing to consider as it relates to reputation is self-promotion. King David did not go around reminding everyone how awesome he was. He did not tell people he was great. They experienced his greatness for themselves. He let others become his publicists and ambassadors. Whenever I contribute to someone's life, they tell others; I never have to say anything. Remember, there is no self-promotion with greatness!

What is your reputation? Ask three people who know you or have conducted business with you to give three words to describe your reputation. Ask them to please answer honestly. The answers may surprise you. Remember, if you don't like what you hear, it is never too late to change yourself.

CHASING GREATNESSgment>

*Name:*_____ *Relationship:* _____
What three words describe my reputation?

1) _____ 2)_____ 3) _____

*Name:*_____ *Relationship:* _____
What three words describe my reputation?

1) _____ 2)_____ 3) _____

*Name:*_____ *Relationship:* _____
What three words describe my reputation?

1) _____ 2)_____ 3) _____

Boldness

Being bold means one must not hesitate or show fear in the face of danger. Boldness engages three components—courage, bravery, and confidence: a. the courage to make up your mind or spirit to face difficulty, b. the bravery to move physically toward your goal while you face difficulty, c. the confidence to fully trust and rely upon Christ. Several people in the Bible demonstrated boldness in the face of controversy:

- David when he killed the giant Goliath (1 Samuel 17:45-49);
- Daniel when he defied the King's law to pray to the King and not God (Daniel 6:10-23);

12

- The Hebrew men (Shadrack, Meshach, and Abednego) when they refused to serve other gods (Daniel 3:8-18);

- Peter and John when they insisted on speaking and teaching in the name of Jesus (Acts 4:13-31);

- Paul when he preached in the name of Jesus and risked his own life for the Gospel (Acts 9:27-29).

A life without living beyond traditional expectation isn't really living; it is existing. In fact, others often avoid bold people because boldness challenges us. In the midst of boldness, complacency is not optional. Bold people force us to live in the sphere of greater expectation, to believe in the impossible. I welcome boldness in every aspect of my life, professionally and personally. I embrace my bold clients, colleagues, and friends. They are highly capable and confident. And yes, sometimes they are frustrating; but in the quest for greatness, I'd rather surround myself with bold comrades than timid cowards who will not push me into my greatness. It is important to note that being rude and having no tact are not the same as being bold.

If I want everyone to like me, boldness is not a trait I should develop. Boldness often requires going against the grain, which can be difficult in our *"go along to get along"* society. The greats (Rosa Parks, Gandhi, Mitch Snyder, Susan B. Anthony, Malcolm X, Dr. Martin Luther King, Jr., and Billy Graham, among others) never went along with the crowd for convenience. All spoke up and acted with boldness. Greatness demands boldness.

Good Judgment

"How much better to get wisdom than gold, and good judgment than silver!" (Proverbs 16:16, NLT). Good judgment involves weighing the consequences before engaging in the act. It sounds simple enough, right? Wrong! Have you noticed, the simplest things are often the most difficult? Sometimes it is hard to walk away from a relationship that is clearly not in your best interest, or to return the shoes you cannot afford, or to avoid that brownie when you are trying to lose those extra pounds.

Good judgment is applying experience and knowledge to difficult circumstances. Good judgment engages several factors one might consider, including:

- Will God be illuminated by my decision?
- What is the law as it pertains to this situation?
- What are my moral values?
- What is my depth of experience?
- Am I excellent in this arena?
- How will this impact me and/or others?
- What does my conscience or gut say?
- Does my education qualify me to make this decision?
- Under what circumstances will I fail?
- Under what circumstances will I succeed?
- Am I tired or hungry?
- Do I need more time?

- Will I feel the same in three days?
- Will I feel the same in a year?

Our emotions are the critical juncture of history and judgment—history from past experiences and judgment from our personal understanding of right and wrong. Do you value your emotions over solid, good judgment? While our circumstances change daily, our changing emotions need special consideration. Life often calls for us to suppress our emotions to make the best decisions, yet often this is not acknowledged.

I was 27 when my best friend asked to borrow $50,000 for a real estate investment. I was pressured relentlessly. Finally I acquiesced, but not without a promissory note, the deed to one of his properties, and a legal contract. Needless to say, the loan went sour and so did the friendship. Two years later, he repaid the loan and the attorney fees, but the friendship was lost. In hindsight, I realize I never felt completely secure in my decision. Why did I give in to my friend's petitions? My conscience said no, but I gave in because of his persistent pressuring and my emotional desire to please a friend despite my better judgment. Not long after I loaned the money, I heard Oprah say three words that would resound in my spirit for years to come: *"Doubt means Don't!"*

My friend later told me he gambled the money away. I couldn't believe it—someone so law-abiding, focused, respected, and grounded. *How could he?* But the more important question was, *Why did I make the loan?* After much reflection, I realized my emotions made the loan, not my better judgment. Emotions cost me a close friendship and two years to recover $50,000 of my net worth.

Prayer

I was spiritually prompted to write this book years before I put pen to paper. I knew the book would be a valuable guide for young professionals—for anyone, really—moving through corporate politics while managing their personal lives. For months I prayed about the details: *Where would I find the time to write a book? Who would publish it? Where would I go for peace and quiet? How would I pay my bills if I moved away?*...So many questions, but no immediate answers. After months of praying and planning, God said, *"Go to London."* *What?! London is twice as expensive as the United States and full of distractions.*

With God, you always acquiesce. God answered my prayers and provided the opportunity and resources for me to move to London. I had no idea what to expect. My emotions were fear and anxiety, but I trusted God wanted me in London. The more I moved toward God, the more steps God took toward me. Like any *healthy* relationship, the more you trust, the more the other person trusts. God loves those who trust Him. Psalm 34:9b (NIV) says, "Fear the Lord, you his saints, for those who fear him lack nothing." Trusting in God builds your greatness muscles and strengthens your good judgment. Likewise, not trusting in God only builds your negative emotions.

After I returned from London, God continued to woo me. Several weeks later, I received a call from a radio station manager who wanted to discuss an opportunity. I was intrigued, so I agreed to meet the following week. In the meeting, the station manager remarked about how much he respected my work in ministry, the excellence of our team, and our business acumen. He went on to say that he wanted to know if I would be interested in hosting a radio show for the station. Now, of course I was beaming from ear to ear. My emotions said, "Yes, yes, yes!" but, first things first. I had to pray. Good opportunities are not always God opportunities. Opportunities either *distract you from* or *deliver you toward* your purpose. Assessing an opportunity should seldom be based on unreconciled emotion, but must be based on the good judgment we outlined earlier. More importantly, every opportunity should include prayer. My personal prayer process involves:

- Surrendering to the prayer process;
- Surveying my emotions by realizing *God's desire,* not *my desire*;
- Determining the best Godly outcome;
- Confirmation through circumstance, people, provision, or proclamation.

Prayer is a petition to God and should be the foundation for every decision. It is through our communication with God, our prayers, that we convey our desire and God reveals His purpose and will for our lives. After prayer I said yes to the radio program.

Chapter Highlights

- Greatness is the collision of character and service.
- We each take an active role in our destiny, whether intentional or not.
- Our lives are a culmination of circumstances and situations that may have carried us to places we *don't want* to be—life happening to us and not us happening to life.
- God uniquely designed us individually for His purpose. If God has set you apart and reveres you, why should you want to be a clone of someone else?

- We've become a society of imitators, not innovators. Imitators model someone else. Innovators create their own mold.

- Your reputation is what people say about you, good or bad.

- Reputation is less about what you think of yourself and more about how and what you communicate to others.

- There is no self-promotion with greatness. Let other people become your publicists and ambassadors.

- Boldness involves three components: courage, bravery, and confidence.

- A life without living beyond traditional expectation is not really living. It is existing.

- Our emotions are the critical juncture of history and judgment—history from past experiences and judgment from personal understanding of right and wrong.

- Good judgment involves weighing the consequences before engaging in the act, and applying experience and knowledge to difficult circumstances.

- Trusting in God builds your greatness muscles and strengthens your good judgment. Likewise, not trusting in God builds only your emotions.

- Good opportunities are not always God opportunities.

- Nothing supersedes prayer.

UP NEXT ⇨

Virtues in Greatness shows how to display humility instead of pride, kindness instead of envy, forgiveness instead of wrath, diligence instead of sloth, charity instead of greed, self-control instead of gluttony, and chastity instead of lust.

Virtues in Greatness

Virtues	Sin
Humility	Pride
Kindness	Envy
Patience	Wrath
Diligence	Sloth
Charity	Greed
Self Control	Gluttony
Chastity	Lust

vs.

CHAPTER 2
Virtues in Greatness

Our culture celebrates rich young drug starlets, gang banger rappers, women who kiss and tell, satanic rock stars, and women with big breasts and little brains. According to a poll on pollingpoint.com, 60% of parents say the behavior of famous people influences the behavior of *their teenagers* (http://www.pollingpoint.com/result/25). In fact, if you ask most young professionals whom they admire, they applaud people with prestigious jobs and money. They rarely cite character traits. What happened to respecting or emulating the traits of people who changed lives, built dreams, and impacted destinies? What happened to celebrating people who did so with strong virtues? Although we may never verbalize it, I wonder if our society really sees a benefit to virtue. **Yet virtues are the foundation of greatness.**

Sin never produces the greatness God intended for us. Patience and self-control help me avoid strangling crazy clients. Kindness has opened doors referrals could not. Humility and respect help people feel engaged and comfortable, and once people feel comfortable they offer greater personal and professional insight. No great thing has happened to anyone who did not embrace the virtues listed in the diagram on the facing page.

For every virtue, there is a sin. Sin is doing what feels good regardless of who gets hurt and what's sacrificed. Virtues say, *How can I serve you?* Sin says, *How can I serve me?* Virtue takes us to greatness, but sin distances us from greatness. In this chapter, we examine each virtue and assess areas we can improve.

Chastity

When people hear "chastity," immediately they think *sexless*. Chastity means more than saying no to sex; it is embracing moral wholesomeness. In a time when the media beckons us to engage in the forbidden and when moral character is placed second to publicity, chastity is the high road for our inherited frailties. **A chaste life is one of moral consciousness, not perfection.** Chastity is demonstrated in our dress, looks, verbal and nonverbal communication, and unspoken intentions. It takes the moral high ground, demonstrated in our respect for self and others. Chastity is essential to a life of commitment to the greater good. It gives and earns respect.

Any form of abstinence is a massive exercise in self-control, another virtue we'll address further along in the chapter. When we tell the world we don't respect abstinence, what we're saying is we don't value self-control.

Although we may not always want to be chaste, I know we need it; the chaos in the world shows us that.

Deuteronomy 10:12-13 (NLT) says it all: "And now, Israel, what does the Lord your God require of you? He requires only that you fear the Lord your God, and live in a way that pleases him, and love him and serve him with all your heart and soul. And you must always obey the Lord's commandments and decrees that I am giving you today for your own good." I love the last part, *"for your own good."* Everything God requires is for our good. We fight so hard with God, but when we do it our way, the results seldom yield greatness. **Greatness has a requirement—virtue.** Without a virtuous life, you are unlikely to be victorious in greatness.

When I first became a Christian and for sometime after that, I was out of control—drinking, smoking, and partying. I was working at BET and had all access to VIP parties and nightspots. I loved it. I was young, cute, and stupid. Today I'm a long way from that young woman who danced till 5 a.m. and went to work three hours later. I'm more honest about where I am emotionally and spiritually, not trying to impress, only trying to improve. I don't make excuses about my struggles. I don't call people judgmental because they are somewhere I am not. It's amazing how we accept God's word as truth but fight against God's order. I try to live by Psalm 119:133 (KJV), which says, "Order my steps in thy word: and let not any iniquity have dominion over me." Dominion is power or possession over me.

God's word is Truth *in its entirety*. You can't pick and choose what fits your life. I used to say, "I'll take a lot of those blessings but not the chastity. I'll take gifts, but I don't want any of that trusting-God stuff." But God's word is not a buffet. **We can't practice buffet Bible and**

expect bountiful blessings. My prayer is, *God keep me so that my lack of integrity doesn't compromise my destiny and greatness.* Nothing super-long and extra-saintly; simply that I walk a life where people see God in me. Chastity is God's order, but in order to attain chastity we must have self-control or we are powerless.

Self-Control

Self-control is another virtue in greatness. **Self-control is restraint over one's own will or personal self—behavior, actions, and thoughts.** When I was trying to lose some extra pounds, God poignantly laid on my heart that my lack of self-control was directly related to my weight gain. An increase in self-control leads to decreased pounds on the scale. The reverse is also true. With a decrease in self-control, I eat whatever I want; I go for the immediate gratification of the food, and I gain weight.

During times when our feelings cause us to vacillate, self-control is a necessary step toward greatness and maintaining our focus. There is no greatness without self-control. The biblical description of self-control is as follows:

WITHOUT SELF-CONTROL YOU:
- Will become lost and eventually die (Proverbs 5:23);
- Will have no protection (Proverbs 25:28);
- Are foolish (Proverbs 5:23);
- Hate everything that is good (2 Timothy 3:3).

SELF-CONTROL WILL:

- Bring knowledge (2 Peter 1:6);

- Bring patience (2 Peter 1:6);

- Bring godliness (2 Peter 1:6);

- Expose sin (Act 24:25);

- Bring an everlasting crown or reward (1 Corinthians 9:25);

- Know no boundaries (Galatians 5:23);

- Guide you through life (Proverbs 6:23).

Self-control is the cornerstone virtue for all other virtues. Self-control is the most important because it's the nucleus of strong character.

Second Timothy 3:1-4 seems to sum up our current society and its lack of self-control. It reads, "But mark this: There will be terrible times in the last days. People will be lovers of themselves, lovers of money, boastful, proud, abusive, disobedient to their parents, ungrateful, unholy, without love, unforgiving, slanderous, without *self-control*, brutal, not lovers of the good, treacherous, rash, conceited, lovers of pleasure rather than lovers of God" (NIV).

It's sad yet amazing to see God's word so closely resemble our society today. We like immediate gratification, yet despise the long-term consequences. Self-control doesn't yield immediate fleshly satisfaction, but it does contribute to greatness.

Charity

According to Winston Churchill, "We make a living by what we get, but we make a life by what we give." Charity, often referred to as philanthropy, involves donating money, goods, time, or effort to support a charitable cause, usually over an extended period of time with a defined objective. The word "philanthropy" is from the Greek, meaning *love for mankind.*

Last year I had the pleasure of attending *Building Your Business in Stilettos*®, a mini-conference for women interested in starting their own businesses. It was delightful to see so many novice and seasoned businesswomen. There were many sessions, excellent networking opportunities, and lots of resources. My favorite highlight from the conference was when the co-founder said, "Some of us need bigger goals than buying shoes." I concur. We spend so much time on superficial things. Perhaps it's to fill our own personal esteem. But charity makes a life of greatness.

Philippians 2:3-4 (NIV) says, "Do nothing out of selfish ambition or vain conceit, but in humility consider others better than yourselves. Each of you should look not only to your own interests, but also to the interests of others." So, what does charity look like to you?_____

_____

_____

In my opinion, no other group has managed a better systematic way of giving than the Jewish Community. *Tzedakah* is a Hebrew word commonly translated as charity and refers to the religious obligation to perform charity, philanthropic acts, which Judaism emphasizes as important to a spiritual life. Unlike philanthropy, which is completely voluntary, *Tzedakah* must be performed regardless of financial standing, even by poor people. If people can't donate money, they contribute in other ways. They can donate clothes, spend time with sick or lonely people, etc. Giving is even ranked from best to worst:

- Giving and enabling the recipient to become self-reliant;
- Giving when neither party knows the other's identity;
- Giving when you know the recipient's identity, but he doesn't know yours;
- Giving when you don't know the recipient's identity, but he knows yours;
- Giving before being asked;
- Giving after being asked;
- Giving less than you should, but giving it happily;
- Giving begrudgingly.

When you look at the needs in our community, country, and world, giving can be challenging, and whom to give to, overwhelming. *Tzedakah* ranks the priority of our giving based on the following model:

1. Family and close relatives
2. Local Jewish community
3. Jewish community in Israel
4. Jewish communities worldwide
5. Local community in general
6. International assistance to needy people

I have challenged the Spiritually Speaking subscribers of my online ministry to stop excessive spending and develop a philanthropic strategy that engages the needs of their family, community, and special interests. I challenge you as well to find something you are passionate about and give. **Charitable giving is critical to a fulfilling life marked by greatness.**

Children's organizations were an obvious area for me to consider. I love children and feel a special compassion toward them. Children have no power in their circumstances, and many struggle as the result of poor adult decisions. In addition to financial contributions to several children's organizations, I developed a program to assist 12- to 21-year-old girls with the transition into adulthood. The program, Mentoring and Inspiring Sisters for Success (MISS), is a five-year program with several tracks in finance, health, professional etiquette, and life strategy. MISS pairs dynamic women of various cultures and professional backgrounds with at-risk teens. The program offers intense mentoring in areas that can have the greatest impact on life success.

Where are you in your charity efforts? Answer these questions:

What social causes are you passionate about? _____

_____

_____

What charitable organizations do you currently contribute time or money to?

_____

_____

What more can you do to assist people in need, stop injustice, and/or change the world?_____

_____

_____

What community will your philanthropic efforts serve?_____

_____

_____

To develop strong philanthropic strategies, consider the following:

- Determine a monetary amount or percentage of income you want to give to causes/charities.

- Volunteer and match your time with your money.

- Engage family and friends in "give back" opportunities.

- Sponsor a friend, family member, or co-worker in their charitable efforts.

- Become a catalyst for change by highlighting your efforts to family and friends.

- Promote your cause by tagging your voicemail message or email signatures.

- Ask your human resources department about their philanthropic efforts. Many companies have budgets for corporate donations.

Tikkun Olam is a Hebrew phrase that means "repairing the world" or "perfecting the world." Implement Tikkun Olam in your life's purpose, your goals, even your relationships. Charitable giving enhances the life of the giver as much as that of the recipient.

Diligence

Are you the person working hard, or the person hardly working? To be diligent is to be hard-working, not lazy. Dictionary.com defines **diligent as constant in effort to accomplish something; attentive and persistent in doing anything.** It's unfortunate that few people want to work hard today. Employees slack off with too many coffee and cigarette breaks. Parents spend fewer and fewer hours at work and less time with their children. We sit at restaurant tables and pack on 30 pounds but when it's time to hit the gym, we're too tired…but never too tired to eat. And when we *finally* get to the gym, we want the hot body in just three weeks.

My greatest tips for being diligent are to change the mindset, choose a target, have a plan, avoid distractions, and recognize and reward successes.

Change the mindset. Developing diligence usually requires a change of mind. Change begins with me. We have to decide we want to see a change. Many things may come against me, but it's ultimately up to me to succeed. If I don't change my mind, I can't be diligent. I listen to people who struggle with their finances. The successful ones always say the same thing. They made the decision to stop spending and start saving. They changed their minds and that changed their behavior. It's that simple.

Choose a target. Diligence needs a goal or a focus—a target. The desire for the target must be stronger than the difficulty of the task itself. Desire must overpower the difficulty. Visualize the target. What does my new body look like? What does a man who loves me and treats me with respect look like? What does a woman who supports and encourages my dream look like?

Have a plan. A plan is simply a roadmap to the target. The plan keeps us on target. Set a plan and keep at it, one step at a time. Include timeframes and keep a daily or weekly journal to mark progress. Enlist the assistance of experts. Credit counselors give plans for decreasing debts; personal trainers give plans for achieving fitness goals; career counselors assess your employment opportunities. Diligence requires a plan.

Avoid distractions. Every day comes with a new set of temptations. As soon as I try to engage in a plan to be diligent, I am immediately tempted. I start my new diet in the morning and receive a dinner invitation tonight. Make a plan to overcome these distractions and temptations by having counterattacks ready. How will I respond to the temptation? I have a script. When someone calls for dinner, I say, "Let's go to the gym instead," or, "I'm on a budget and it doesn't include eating out." Having a counterattack beforehand is easier than trying to come up with something on the spot. **Temptations come to test how serious and committed we are to our target.** Practice counterattacks; be ready.

Recognize and reward success. As you achieve your goals, you become encouraged. When I reach even small achievable goals, I celebrate. When I lose ten pounds, I get super-charged to lose the rest. Success breeds success. Reward yourself each time you get closer to your target(s).

We must have an aggressive attitude when developing diligence. Answer these questions:

What would you like to be more diligent about? _____

_____

_____

What is your target? _____
_____
_____

What are potential distractions and temptations? _____
_____
_____

How do you plan to overcome these distractions and temptations? ____
_____
_____

What small milestones will you recognize and reward? _____
_____
_____

Patience

Many of us can't wait in a checkout line for ten minutes without fidgeting non-stop. **Patience is waiting without anxiety.** The dictionary also refers to patience as "staying power." It's trusting in God to deliver even when we don't know the outcome, and doing so without grumbling. In my personal romantic relationships, I wish my options were more expansive. In my impatience, I could connect myself with someone who isn't God's best choice for me and be married tomorrow. But I am patient and wait for God's best. When we wait on God's best, we exercise greater trust in Him than in humanity or ourselves. **Patience is the intersection of what God has for us and what we believe for ourselves.** Here are three things God teaches about patience:

Patience is the fruit of the Holy Spirit (Galatians 5:22). Patience is the ability to bear trials without grumbling. **Patience must be embraced as a mindset, before it can be engaged as an action.** Not only is patience a virtue, it's also one of the gifts of the Spirit along with love, joy, peace, kindness, goodness, faithfulness, gentleness, and self-control. The more we grow in our relationship with God, the more fruit we yield. Fruit is simply another name for productivity. Just like our job requires us to produce, so does God. Where we are spiritually determines how much fruit we produce. Ineffective leaders are usually the result of lack of focus, impulsiveness, unproductiveness, and limited fruit.

Patience is required for God to fulfill His promises (Hebrews 6:12). Recently I reread Kay Arthur's book *Lord, Teach Me to Pray in 28 Days*. In the book, Kay asks readers to write down their prayer goals. When I opened the book, I saw my old prayer list written there: confirmation of my purpose, to move abroad, write a book, grow the Spiritually Speaking program, and speak in tongues. A year later God had met all my prayer requests—all. Some of the items on my list I had forgotten about until I reopened Kay's book. **When we are patient, God can really fulfill His promises and blow our minds.** Likewise, we can demonstrate our love for God by waiting with patience for Him to act.

God's patience allows our salvation (2 Peter 3:15). God's patience waits for us because He loves us so much. I remember when I was a teenager, my boyfriend said, "If you love me, then you will have sex with me." I was strong enough even then to say, "If you love me, then you will wait." God says the same thing: "If you love me, you will wait. My love for you is demonstrated in my patience. Likewise, you can demonstrate your love for Me by waiting with patience for Me to act." While we were still sinners,

God sent His Son to die for us. He knew that in due time, we would come to Him. *Due time…* patience!

Below, write a few things you are waiting for.
Pray now for God to help you persevere with patience.
Thank Him for being patient with you.

_____

_____

_____

_____

_____

Kindness

Colossians 3:12 (NIV) says, "Therefore as God's chosen people, holy and dearly loved, clothe yourselves with compassion, kindness, humility, gentleness and patience." **Kindness requires compassion, friendship, and sympathy.** For naturally happy and joyous people, kindness comes easy. For others, kindness requires more intention.

Several years ago I had a reputation for berating others. In fact, I'm still working to mend some fragile relationships. Now I realize that when I put the needs of others before my own, they respond in kind. Everyone wins. With kindness, I've formed political and spiritual allies. **Kindness builds others up.** Here are some character traits of kindness:

- Kindness and mercy are companions (Exodus 33:19);
- You are blessed when you are kind (Proverbs 14:21);

- You give honor to God when you are kind (Proverbs 14:31);

- God rewards the kind (Proverbs 28:8);

- God's promises bring kindness (2 Kings 13:23);

- Kindness provides protection from God's wrath (1 Samuel 15:6);

- Lack of kindness hurts others (Psalm 109:16);

- God's kindness brings wisdom and insight (Ephesians 1:8);

- Kindness brings people to Christ (1 Timothy 1:14);

- Our words should be seasoned with kindness (1 Colossians 4:6).

According to Ephesians 4:32, kindness is a demonstration of love. First Corinthians 13:4 tells us that love is kind, and then goes on to say, love is not jealous or boastful or proud. I know I've never been in love because every relationship I've had doesn't fit this definition.

The Southern saying, "You can catch more flies with honey than vinegar," is true. Kindness is like honey. Be kind and use your honey…honey!

How can you express more kindness in your relationships?

Name	How will you show this person kindness?
_____	_____
_____	_____
_____	_____
_____	_____
_____	_____

List the people you've been unkind to in the past. How will you make amends?

_____

_____

_____

_____

_____

Humility

The Hebrew word for *humble* is "to become low." **Humility is giving credit without glorifying self or expecting anything in return.** A humble spirit is a prized possession in heaven.

I learned some lessons about humility while working at BET. During the peak of my career, I was responsible for setting up national events, parties, screenings, concerts—you name it and I planned it. My signature uniform was jeans, sneakers, t-shirt, and a baseball cap. It was comfortable and inconspicuous. Once I was planning an NBA All-Star post-game celebrity party. This particular party was the hottest party of the weekend. I controlled who got in and who did not. The VIP list was mine and I was its master. I was at the front door when two ladies entered and completely disregarded me. Perhaps it was my low-key uniform, or my easy-going personality; whatever the case, they didn't realize they needed to go through me. Perturbed by their arrogance, I did allow them to enter but not without cautioning them about their disrespect. I wonder if this is how God feels when we ignore Him.

Exercising constant humility is the best way to guarantee entrance to the Kingdom. **Humility is God's Spirit showing through us and manifesting in our lives to impact other people. Pride and stubbornness prevent us from exercising humility.** Our humility brings God recognition and glory. We need to come to our brokenness or lower place, where we end and God begins. It takes a special person to lower themselves, especially if that humility builds someone else up. Not only are Christians to be humble in a few things, but according to Ephesians 4:2, we are to be humble in *all* we do. Look at the promises for the humble:

Humility brings wisdom (Proverbs 11:2);

Humility brings Godly promotion (Luke 14:11, 18:14);

Humility brings Godly grace (1 Peter 5:6).

I couldn't sum up the virtue of humility without examining 2 Chronicles 7:14 (NIV), "If my people, who are called by my name, will *humble themselves* and pray and seek my face and turn from their wicked ways, then will I hear from heaven and will forgive their sin and will heal their land." We see here several key components of humility: bringing ourselves low, praying, seeking God's face, and departing from sin. Then God will hear us and heal us.

Are you humble? What does your humility look like?

In what areas do you struggle with pride and arrogance? List them here.

_____

_____

Pick one and develop a plan for implementing humility.

_____

_____

All seven virtues express God's desire for His children. Without a strong foundation and understanding of these virtues, greatness cannot be obtained. When we embrace these virtues, we see the manifestation in our spiritual growth. Complete this exercise before moving to the next chapter.

Virtue	How can you improve each virtue?
Chastity	
Self-control	
Charity	
Diligence	
Patience	
Kindness	
Humility	

Chapter Highlights

- Virtues are the foundation of greatness.
- Sin never produces the greatness God intended for us.
- A chaste life is one of moral consciousness, not perfection.

- Greatness has a requirement—virtue.

- God's word is Truth in its entirety.

- Chastity is demonstrated in our dress, looks, verbal and nonverbal communication, and unspoken intentions.

- Charitable giving is critical to a fulfilling life marked by greatness.

- Diligence is a constant effort to accomplish something—being attentive and persistent in doing anything.

- My greatest tips for being diligent are to change the mindset, choose a target, have a plan, avoid distractions, and recognize and reward successes.

- Self-control is restraint over one's own will or personal self—behavior, actions, and thoughts.

- Temptations come to test how serious and committed we are to our target.

- Patience is waiting without anxiety.

- Patience is the intersection of what God has for us and what we believe for ourselves.

- Patience must be embraced as a mindset before it can be engaged as an action.

- When we are patient, God can really fulfill His promises and blow our minds.

- Our lives should marry God's intention and our effort.

- Humility is God's spirit showing through us and manifesting in our lives to impact other people.

- Pride and stubbornness prevent us from exercising humility.

- Charity, often referred to as philanthropy, involves donating money, goods, time, or effort to support a charitable cause, usually over an extended period of time with a defined objective.

- Patience is waiting without anxiety; staying power; and trusting God more than the circumstances while you wait.

- Kindness requires compassion, friendship, and sympathy. Kindness builds others up.

- Humility is giving credit without glorifying self or expecting anything in return. It takes a special person to lower themselves, especially if that humility builds someone else up.

UP NEXT ⇨

Greatness Grabbers Part I: Seduction of Sin outlines tools, tips, and tricks to make confrontation mutually beneficial.

Greatness Grabbers

Part I: Seduction of Sin

CHAPTER 3
Greatness Grabbers
Part I: Seduction of Sin

Virtues	Sin
Humility	Pride
Kindness	Envy
Patience	Wrath
Diligence	Sloth
Charity	Greed
Self Control	Gluttony
Chastity	Lust

VS.

Some of us are lost; others are misguided. If you don't care, you're lost!

Sin is the jealous mistress of your relationship with God. The sin mistress prohibits a solid marriage between you and the Lord and wants you all to herself. Her goal is to destroy the relationship you have with God by slowly eroding your commitment. Instead of directly using the beautiful full lips or diesel abs, sin's seduction is less blatant but more enticing. **Sin and greatness cannot dwell indefinitely in the same place.**

Each sin has a consequence that hinders our access to greatness. Sometimes it takes one indiscretion to ruin a lifetime of accomplishments; other times, it could take years before an indiscretion is uncovered. Regardless of the duration, the outcome is all the same—shame and the loss of influence. Sin is never worth the cost. The sooner we accept and live by that, the better off we'll be. We can all think of countless politicians, and even preachers, who ruined their reputations because of one or more of the "seven deadly sins." Yet all is not lost; sin can be managed.

The more we pursue God, the less sin manifests in our lives, and the greater our impact in the world. Eventually we begin to see things from a spiritual perspective and not a worldly one.

To illustrate this point, I want to share my acronym for SIN: **SIN is being Spiritually Inept to say No.** How many times have we crossed the threshold of *I know I'm wrong, but just this one time?*

You know you have a proper relationship with God when there is conflict between sin and the Spirit. It's the battle between the conscience and the Holy Spirit—the Holy Spirit convicts us before we sin, and our conscience convicts us after we sin.

We are influenced toward or away from sin in three different ways: Christ, Sin, and Us (our flesh). Look at the diagrams below. As sin increases, God decreases (Stage 1). When God increases, sin decreases (Stage 3). Most of us are probably somewhere in the middle (Stage 2), but our job is to move toward Stage 3.

Stage 1

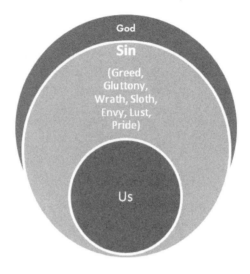

Stage 2

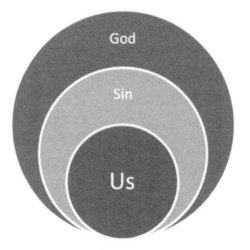

Stage 3

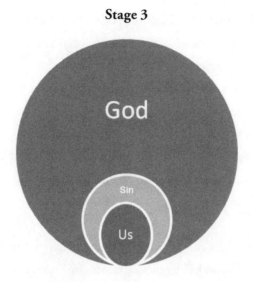

Let's be honest: sin feels good to our flesh. I don't believe we struggle with what to do spiritually. We know. Our struggle is the motivation to change. Hopefully, the tools below will increase our desire *not* to sin.

Self-awareness is the key to knowing what you are capable of and why. This enhanced self-awareness leads to greater spiritual growth, and greater spiritual growth to greatness. As we move toward greatness, we will have to confront the sin in others and ourselves. I offer a practical approach to assessing sin in our lives.

Confrontation

Confrontation forces us to reconcile where we are with where we want to be. We can't change who we are unless we face the truth. Some people would rather live a lie than be confronted with the truth. **To live life**

falsely is to live life less abundantly. Confrontation forces us to look at ourselves and others authentically. There have been times when I've had to confront myself and others. Confronting friends and family members comes at a price, sometimes costing even the relationship. But it's necessary to ensure our environment is fertile for creating an atmosphere that stimulates and fertilizes greatness, not sin. The difference between immature and mature people is that mature people are willing to confront and make the necessary changes to evolve. A person who can't handle confrontation is often quick to refute without listening—a blatant sign of immaturity.

Maturity says, if others confront me, they care enough to enhance my character and integrity. Now I welcome confrontation rather than the uncomfortable, irritating silence when an issue is left unresolved. But there are people who can't handle confrontation.

PEOPLE WHO CANNOT HANDLE CONFRONTATION TEND TO:

- Talk at you and not with you;
- Tune you out after you say something they don't like;
- Be quick to end the conversation;
- Conclude relationships abruptly;
- Get angered easily;
- Not listen attentively;
- Have voice tones that get higher or lower when irritated;
- Be extremely emotional and irrational in their arguments;
- Not be practical.

Confrontation can be difficult for passive, and even for assertive, personalities, but the tools below should offer some assistance.

TOOLS FOR CONFRONTING SIN:

- **Pray.** Ask God to guide you on the timing of the conversation, the words to use. Some confrontations are going to be difficult. At least with prayer you can walk in God's peace.

- **Keep a Conversational Tone of Voice.** This keeps you in control of your emotions. Purposefully plan not to raise or lower your voice. Make your words intentional and direct, but not condescending.

- **Bring the Conversation Back to Them.** Center the conversation on their opinions. Let them speak 70% of the time; you speak 30% and listen 100%. Hear their grievances.

- **Eye Contact.** Eye-to-eye contact demonstrates that you are engaged. When you look away, it means you are not. Don't even blink. Just kidding!—but keep eye contact when you do.

- **Past vs. Pattern.** Gather three or more key points. People don't like you bringing up the past, but tell them it's not about their past; it's about their pattern.

- **Examples & Evidence.** Gather three or more supporting examples or pieces of evidence. It is difficult to challenge the truth. Repeat several times in different ways to ensure they get the point.

- **End on a High Note.** End the confrontation positively. For example, if the conversation with a coworker gets heated, let them know what you respect and admire about them. Make sure they know the subject you've been discussing is not your permanent opinion of them, but an observation. *Good, bad, good* should be the structure of the confrontation. For example: *John, your customer service is excellent. However, your tardiness is bringing some complaints from other departments. We need to ensure that the mailroom is open on time to receive early deliveries. Being punctual will enhance your excellent customer service skills.*

- **Outcome**. What do you want the final outcome to be? Let the other person know the desired outcome before you confront.

Now that we've looked at sin in general and confrontation as a tool for addressing it, let's examine the "seven deadly sins"—lust, gluttony, greed, sloth, wrath, envy, and pride.

#1 LUST Lust is an inordinate craving for pleasure of the body. Lust is one sin that is not victimless. Eventually it entangles others. The sin of lust usually begins with the eyes. Matthew 5:28 (NLT) says, "But I say, anyone who even looks at a woman with lust has already committed adultery with her in his heart." Again, Proverbs 27:20 (KJV) says, "Hell and destruction are never full; so the eyes of man are never satisfied." Greatness and lust cannot coexist; one will eventually win. Sin is on the increase because spiritual growth is on the decline. Simply put, sin is more enticing because people are less spiritual.

Lust continues to escalate in our society that says you can have it all, even if it belongs to someone else...*take their money, pursue her husband, and seduce his wife.* New media forms deliver lust at our fingertips. The seductions of sex, fame, money, and power are in your mailbox, on television, or a click away. First John 2:16 (KJV) sums it up well: "For all that is in the world, the lust of the flesh, and the lust of the eyes, and the pride of life, is not of the Father, but is of the world." I've learned to control my lust before someone comes along to satisfy it.

Desire without boundaries is emotional anarchy. Many people have lustful thoughts, but how we manage these thoughts will determine our level of greatness. When I see a handsome man, my mind can wander everywhere. In a matter of seconds I can go from undressing him with my eyes…to foreplay and the grand finale—*mind play*. I stop myself as soon as the first thought comes and pray to God; my spirit kills the thought. Thoughts submitted to God and subjected to His word will help control lust and keep us out of trouble, but the heart has to be willing. The desire to sin is no more absent from a Christian than it is from a non-Christian. The only difference is the Christian's awareness and dedication *not* to sin—hopefully, anyway.

Lust dis-empowers and needs to be counteracted with something more powerful, the pursuit of Christ. This pursuit of becoming more Christ-like is called sanctification, but sanctification is a progression. Not so long ago, I met a handsome youth pastor who said he had conquered his lust for women. He was thirty-one, a virgin, and did I say handsome? He was. He had managed to grow to a place in his sanctification that enabled him to see women as sisters and not objects of his lustful desire. (No, he was not gay.) Wow! I have a long way to go. He told me it was possible. I believe him. I believe him, above all, because *God* says it is possible.

You can't control the acts of others, but you can control yourself. No one gets saved (confesses their sins and says that Jesus Christ is their Lord and Savior) on Tuesday and is without temptation on Thursday. Sanctification is a commitment to wanting to change and a daily conscientious effort to make the change long-term.

When sanctification is at work in our lives, the following happens:

- The heart desires to do the will of God;

- Our purpose is to be a servant of God, not self;

- We are more responsive to the prompting of the Holy Spirit (the desire to do right and be virtuous);

- We have true allegiance to God, not humanity;

- Our mental desires are aligned with our eternal destiny (we think about what we have, not what we need).

Desire doesn't compromise our greatness; lust does. Lust impedes us from reaching our best. We become consumed with the object of our lustful desire instead of with our destiny.

#2 GLUTTONY Gluttony, the second deadly sin, is an inordinate desire to consume more than one requires. Often we think of gluttony as eating too much, but gluttony is unreasonable excess of any kind. Gluttons always want more, especially in our super-sized society...*super-size my car, super-size my house, super-size my boobs, super-size my penis!* When are we going to super-size our spirits?

The need for excess is a progressive and silent killer. Hebrews 13:5 (NIV) cautions against just that: "Keep your lives free from the love of money and be content with what you have, because God has said, 'Never will I leave you; never will I forsake you.'" Ironically, our contentment opens up the door for God to shower us with more blessings. But we have little chance for contentment without first learning to be satisfied with what we do have. Herbert Simon coined the term *satisfice*, a decision-making strategy that calls us to accept what's adequate rather than the optimal. Initially, when I heard this term from my friend Valorie Burton, I was a little underwhelmed. Why would someone want to satisfice and not optimize? By satisficing we opt for the small and not the great. But we don't compromise the dream; we compromise the distractions—distractions like competing, which is a symptom of gluttony. Competing with others leads us to concentrate more on what they have and less on what we need to do long-term. We make movements according to someone else's efforts and not our own, trying to keep up with our friend's career path and not our God-given gifts and talents. Soon we're competing in their arena—an arena never intended for us—and with little success. Contentment is the salve for gluttony. When I become content, I no longer overindulge. I am content without competing.

We see this quite often in friendships. Let's say you have two friends, Angela and Betty. Angela is single and owns a business, a home, and a new luxury car. Betty, on the other hand, had a slow start. She took some wrong turns, married early, and divorced young. Betty tries to make up for lost time by accumulating as much *stuff* as Angela. What Betty doesn't know is that God wants to exceed her expectations and use her life experiences as an opportunity to bless others. God needs Betty's full attention, but Betty can't take the undivided time because she's accumulated so much debt chasing Angela's life and not her own.

If Betty were content and still, God could prepare her for the next level. This doesn't mean Betty will never reach her full potential. It just means there may be a delay. God wants us to be content because it allows Him to prepare us for the next level of living, but we become gluttons when we can't be content where we are and with what we already have.

Philippians 4:11 (KJV) says, "Not that I speak in respect of want: for I have learned, in whatsoever state I am, therewith to be content." Contentment is born of a humble spirit while gluttony wants more, more, more. The sin of gluttony is similar to the third deadly sin, greed.

#3 GREED Greed is an excessive desire for material things, wealth, or gain. The best remedy for greed is giving. Rick Warren, author of the best-selling book *The Purpose Driven Life*, lives off 10% of his income and gives away 90%. I've visited many churches, but unfortunately far too many have the wrong motives with regard to money. Two distinct stories in the Bible address greed and money: the rich ruler who had money but could not surrender his riches to walk fully with God, and the woman with the alabaster jar of perfume who surrendered all. Their stories are recorded here.

The Rich Ruler from Luke 18:18-25 (KJV) says *And a certain ruler asked him, saying, Good Master, what shall I do to inherit eternal life? And Jesus said unto him, Why callest thou me good? None is good, save one, that is, God. Thou knowest the commandments, Do not commit adultery, Do not kill, Do not steal, Do not bear false witness, Honor thy father and thy mother. And he said, All these have I kept from my youth up. Now when Jesus heard these things, he said unto him, Yet lackest thou one thing: sell all that thou hast, and distribute unto the poor, and thou shalt have treasure in heaven: and come, follow me. And when he heard this, he was very sorrowful: for he was very rich. And when Jesus saw that he was very sorrowful, he said, How hardly shall they that have riches enter into the kingdom of God! For it is easier for a camel to go through a needle's eye, than for a rich man to enter into the kingdom of God.*

The Woman with the Alabaster Jar as told in Matthew 26:7-13 (KJV): *There came unto him a woman having an alabaster box of very precious ointment, and poured it on his head, as he sat at meat. But when his disciples saw it, they had indignation, saying, To what purpose is this waste? For this ointment might have been sold for much, and given to the poor. When Jesus understood it, he said unto them, Why trouble ye the woman? For she hath wrought a good work upon me. For ye have the poor always with you; but me ye have not always. For in that she hath poured this ointment on my body, she did it for my burial. Verily I say unto you, Wheresoever this gospel shall be preached in the whole world, there shall also this, that this woman hath done, be told for a memorial of her.*

I have yet to meet a greedy giver. Our giving is a direct contrast to our greed; the greater our giving, the less our greed. Greed is our inability to trust God for supernatural abundance. God can give us our heart's desire and exceed our expectations. We simply have to trust Him to do it. He will give us more than we can even hope for or imagine, but only when we put Him first.

#4 SLOTH Sloth is, in short, laziness; it is the tendency to avoid physical or spiritual work. I see slothfulness play out in many areas. Marriage is probably the most pervasive arena. If couples were as intentional and dedicated to their marriage as they are about their careers and possessions, the divorce rate would probably be much lower.

Over the years, Spiritually Speaking has co-hosted a program called "Married Women Tell All." The program is highly successful and extremely well attended. Women come for candid discussions to improve their marriage. I assemble a panel of Christian women with Godly answers. Each year, panel members vary, but the answers are always the same: marriage takes work! In no other relationship is sloth more damaging than in marriage. Yet, until we transition our mindset from *what has he or she done for me lately?* to *what can I do for him or her today?* we will continue to see the decline of marriages.

We have much to say about this, but it is hard to explain because you are slow to learn. In fact, though by this time you aught to be teachers, you need someone to teach you the elementary truths of God's word all over again. You need milk, not solid food! Anyone who lives on milk being still an infant, is not acquainted with the teaching about righteousness. But solid food is for the mature, who by constant use have trained themselves to distinguish good from evil (Hebrews 5:11-14, NIV). The desire for a more fruitful and powerful life in God begins with getting rid of sloth. Sloth is our lack of effort to take the *next* step toward greatness. It surfaces in every aspect of our lives: our health, our career, our relationships. Sloth is our inability to move forward because we are too lazy to exercise, too lazy to cook for our spouse, too lazy to get involved in the community, and too lazy to put in the work to change.

#5 WRATH There is a misconception that God hates anger, but what God hates is wrath. Wrath is what we do with our anger, the *action* of our angry emotions. It's being so angry we lose control. Wrath causes you to hurt people physically, to be impulsive, to trample on people, and to move to an immediate counterattack without thinking.

God does not want us reacting emotionally to the actions of others. He wants us to respond with wisdom and a gentle spirit. Ephesians 4:26 (KJV) says, "Be ye angry, and sin not: let not the sun go down upon your wrath."

It's possible to be angry and not sin. Righteous anger is unselfish, but sinful anger is selfishly motivated. When we give in to anger, we focus on our own welfare, comfort, or happiness instead of being concerned for the other person or being a good witness for God. Anger is what we feel; wrath is what we do because of our anger.

Those who know me know that I despise trite things, unnecessary conversation, and belaboring a moot point. Well, every now and then in the workplace, there are situations that require a greater level of patience. Recently at a client's office, I was short on patience. With the backdrop of high-strung employees I exploded and commenced a tongue-lashing on colleagues. My anger was warranted but the tongue-lashing—my wrath—was not. Don't follow my poor example; using the suggestions below can keep your boss and your clients happy:

- Be quiet and let the other party speak. If you can control yourself, you can control the situation.

- Be nice. There is a Southern saying: *"Kill them with kindness."* If you are bigger spiritually and emotionally, you become bigger intellectually. If I feel myself or the other person getting out of control, I say, "I see this is getting really emotional, so let's revisit when we calm down."

- Learn to walk away. If I can't control my words, I'm too emotional. Walking away has saved me time, money, and peace of mind.

Wrath never ends well, so use these tools to control the sin of wrath and display the virtue of patience.

#6 ENVY Envy is the desire for another person's status, abilities, or situation. Sometimes when wonderful things happen for me, such as business opportunities, buying an additional home, or having an article written about my work, the envy of others, even friends, overshadows these opportunities and blessings. Learning how to handle the envy of others while maintaining friendships is emotionally difficult. I've had friends who knew I would be an excellent candidate for a position at their firm but who wouldn't recommend me. They were fearful I would steal their thunder or excel beyond them, but what God has for you no one can take away.

Envious people are always sizing others up. They ask the question, *"How did he or she get that?"* What they really want to know is, *why her or him and not me?* What they don't know is that by asking the question, they already have their answer—"it's not for me." Psalm 75:6-7 (KJV) says, "For promotion cometh neither from the east, nor from the west, nor from the south. But God is the judge: he putteth down one, and setteth up another." **Envy is an expression of distrust in God. Why did God give them that and not me?**

A word of caution: comparison is a slow churn to envy. Comparison leads to competitiveness and competitiveness, to envy. Imagine if people stopped comparing and started collaborating; stopped watching others and started seeking God. When we start reforming, transforming, and conforming ourselves to Christ, we become less concerned with other people and what they have. While envy compares, pride says no one else could possibly be better than me.

#7 PRIDE The final deadly sin is pride. The Bible talks about two types of pride: pride in oneself and pride in God. Obviously self-pride is the deadly sin. Also known as vanity, pride is an excessive belief in one's own abilities. Pride causes us to be myopic in our thinking and actions. Pride says, *they need to know who I am, how much I own, what I drive, what I wear, what I do, and how smart I am.* Pride is often used interchangeably with arrogance and haughtiness. Referred to as the sin from which all other sins arise, pride was the precursor to the demise of many, including Satan. Proverbs 16:18 (NLT): "Pride goes before destruction and haughtiness before a fall."

There is nothing worse than the self-proclaimed ramblings of young professionals with a little skill and even less applicable experience, and their stench of pride pollutes the air. At twenty-five I thought my skills could take me anywhere, but I learned that people would quickly opt for someone with less productivity, but more humility. My boastful personality and *I'm smarter than them* tirades became tiresome. My skills couldn't take me to a point where my character had not evolved. Our pride should always be in Christ and not in ourselves. Pride got Satan kicked out of Heaven; don't let it get you kicked out of opportunities.

The cure for pride is humility and the *choice* to be humble. I've heard people say, *she's rich and regular...very down to earth, easy, no fuss.* I've also heard, *she's difficult, pretentious...drama and broke!* Allow your confidence to illuminate your personality and God-given ability, not your pride. Pride offends.

So there we have it—the seven deadly sins: lust, gluttony, greed, sloth, wrath, envy, and pride. Where are you on the virtue scale? Place an x on the lines below to demonstrate where you fit on each continuum.

Virtue	1 Very Virtuous	2 Quite Virtuous	3 Some of Each	4 Not Virtuous Enough	5 Too Often Sinning	Sin
Humility	————————————————————————————————					*Pride*
Kindness	————————————————————————————————					*Envy*
Patience	———————————————————————————————					*Wrath*
Diligence	————————————————————————————————					*Sloth*
Charity	———————————————————————————————					*Greed*
Self-Control	————————————————————————————————					*Gluttony*
Chastity	———————————————————————————————					*Lust*

Please list your best virtues: Please list your greatest sins:

1) _____   1) _____

2) _____   2) _____

3) _____   3) _____

Do you want to change for the best?   ☐ Yes   ☐ No

Pride, envy, wrath, sloth, greed, gluttony, and lust keep us from a closer relation-ship with God, and further from our destiny. Sin is hip, sexy, and dangerous, and so are the consequences. I can't tell you about sin and not offer solutions. Sin is a process. Psalm 1:1 (KJV) reads, "Blessed is the man that walketh not in the counsel of the ungodly, nor standeth in the way of sinners, nor sitteth in the seat of the scornful." Character is directly connected to our virtue; the greater our virtue, the greater our character. Our character can limit or launch us.

There are three phases that take us to the slippery slope of sin: walking, standing, and sitting. Look at these phases and answer the questions.

Phase 1—Walk Not In The Counsel Of The Ungodly

In Phase 1, I speak with people who are not Godly. Although I don't par-ticipate in their activities, I will associate with them. When they start to do things I don't agree with, I excuse myself and politely exit.

Questions:

☐ Are the people I listen to unwise and immoral?

☐ Has my counsel become ungodly?

☐ Do I check my counsel against the Bible?

Phase 2—Nor Stand In The Way Of Sinners

During Phase 2, I participate in conversations with sinners and sometimes even participate in the sin. At this phase, I may be conflicted but not enough to leave. I may not be comfortable there, but I stay. Eventually, I am comfortable in the presence of sinners.

Questions:

☐ Do I choose to be in sinful environments?

☐ Am I comfortable with sin?

Phase 3—Nor Sit In The Seat Of The Scornful

During Phase 3, I'm participating in the sin, not just an innocent bystander. I may even initiate sin.

Question:

☐ At one time, would this environment have made me uncomfortable?

Here's how the Slippery Slope of Sin can play out in my life: I have to guard my interaction with men. I don't fool myself by pretending that I can compete with my flesh; it's a losing battle. Instead, I take practical steps like: no men at my home when I'm alone, no relationships with people who don't support and respect my beliefs, and no drinking and drugs to unleash my inhibitions and vices. I would hate to ruin ten years of dynamic ministry efforts for ten minutes of pleasure. If I didn't have stop guards, I could easily slip into sexual sin. Consider how subtle the progression might be.

Phase 1 / Initially, I speak to a man who is not Godly or spiritually mature. Then, I spend time with him and he gains influence in my life physically and emotionally.

<u>Phase 2 /</u> Attitude precedes behavior—I start thinking he's a nice guy and ignore my previous non-negotiables (things I could never allow) because I'm lonely. Behavior precedes compromise—I go out with the man and before long let the relationship progress emotionally, eventually physically.

<u>Phase 3 /</u> Finally, I fall into sexual sin. Nothing changes the outcome of the Slippery Slope of Sin except strength in God.

GOD

FREE
Moving
<u>toward</u>
God

BOUND
Moving
<u>from</u> God

SIN

The purpose of Satan's temptation is to draw us further away from Christ and, hence, from our greatness. God tests us on what we have, but Satan tempts us with what we want. Our actions show that we are either free or bound. We are either moving toward God or away from God.

Count the Sin Cost

When tempted, consider your Character, Benefits, Loyalty, Position, and God.

Just because we are committed to following God doesn't mean we won't be tempted. The life of Joseph is an example of what happens when we count the cost of what we sacrifice for sin. Joseph was sold into slavery by his brothers at a young age, but during his servitude, he won favor with Potiphar, an officer of Pharaoh—captain of the guard, to be exact—and an Egyptian. Joseph was favored for his good character. During his service, Joseph was propositioned by Potiphar's wife, but his commitment to his position, benefits, loyalty, and God were critical in upholding his character and one we should model.

Genesis 39 (NKJV). *Thus [Potiphar] left all that he had in Joseph's hand, and he did not know what he had except for the bread which he ate. Now Joseph was handsome in form and appearance. And it came to pass after these things that his master's wife cast longing eyes on Joseph, and she said, "Lie with me." But he refused and said to his master's wife, "Look, my master does not know what is with me in the house, and he has committed all that he has to my hand. There is no one greater in this house than I* (**position**), *nor has he kept back anything from me* (**benefits**) *but you, because you are his wife. How then can I do this great wickedness* (**loyalty to Potiphar**), *and sin against God?"* (**spiritual priority**) *So it was, as she spoke to Joseph day by day, that he did not heed her, to lie with her or to be with her. But it happened about this time, when Joseph went into the house to do his work, and none of the men of the house was inside, that she caught him by his garment, saying, "Lie with me." But he left his garment in her hand, and fled and ran outside.*

As we see with Joseph's story, sin beckons us to partake. At times we will certainly lose the battle, but at what cost? Is the momentary pleasure worth the lifetime blemish on your character? Joseph considered his position, *There is no one greater in this house than I*; his benefits, *nor has he kept back anything from me*; loyalty to Potiphar, *because you are his wife. How then can I do this great wickedness;* and most important, his spiritual devotion to God, *sin against God?* Like Joseph, consider your position, benefits, loyalty, but most importantly, consider God. The scripture never says Joseph wasn't tempted; he was simply smart enough to count the cost.

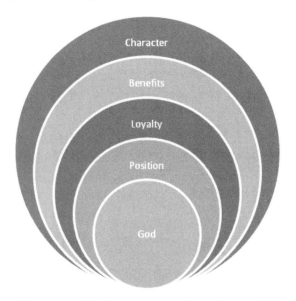

Character: what intangible things are at risk?...what will I lose morally and ethically?

Benefits: what tangible things, financial and perks, are at risk?...what will I lose?...is it worth it?

Loyalty: will I compromise relationships?...can those relationships be repaired?

Position: will I lose favor with my family, friends, job?…will it damage my reputation?

God: most importantly, how will this impact my relationship with God?

The best defense against the sin process is a ready offense. This chapter provided you with an offensive strategy that includes being aware of what the sins are, confronting the sins within yourself, learning to confront them in others, knowing the Slippery Slope of Sin, and understanding how to resist temptation.

What sins do you struggle with?

_____

_____

What will be your strategy when you are confronted with these sins?

_____

_____

Chapter Highlights

- SIN—**S**piritually **I**nept to say **N**o
- Greater spiritual growth increases our opportunity for greatness.
- Confrontation forces us to reconcile where we are with where we want to be.
- Lust is an inordinate craving for pleasure of the body. Lust disempowers and needs to be counteracted with the pursuit of Christ.

- Gluttony is an excessive desire to consume more than one requires. It can be counteracted with satisficing—compromising the small for the great.

- Don't compromise the dream; compromise the distractions.

- Competing with others means we concentrate more on what they have and less on what we need to do.

- Greed is an excessive desire for material things, wealth, or gain. The best remedy for greed is giving.

- Sloth is avoiding physical or spiritual work—laziness. Sloth is our lack of effort to take the *next* step necessary for greatness.

- Wrath is the action of our anger. When we give in to our anger, we often focus on our own welfare, comfort, or happiness instead of the other person's welfare and being a good witness for God.

- Envy is the desire for another person's status, abilities, or situation. Comparison is a slow churn to envy.

- Pride causes us to be myopic in our thinking and actions. The cure for pride is humble power—the choice to act in humility.

- There is a three-step process to sin—walking, standing, and sitting.

- When tempted, consider your character, benefits, loyalty, position, and God.

Up Next ⇨

Greatness Grabbers Part II: From Fear to Lack of Focus explores our own personal deterrents to greatness, including fear, lack of personal awareness, lack of clear expectations, the past, other people's expectations, imperfections, anxiety, lack of follow-through, and lack of focus.

Greatness Grabbers

Part II: From Fear to Lack of Focus

Greatness Grabbers
Part II: From Fear to Lack of Focus

So we've successfully navigated the business world and managed to keep a healthy distance between ourselves and the seven deadly sins. Why then is the greatness not here? In this chapter, we address how we see ourselves. The primary and biggest deterrent to greatness is... our fear of being great.

Fear of Being Great

I love this quote by Marianne Williamson: "Our deepest fear is not that we are inadequate. Our deepest fear is that we are powerful beyond measure" (*A Return to Love: Reflections on the Principles of a Course in Miracles*, Harper Collins, 1992).

We know Moses was a pioneer for the Israelites, but that's not how Moses saw himself. Moses was insecure and afraid. He cites the frailty of his slow speech and even exposes his past and current insecurities. Moses goes on to tell God that, even though God has spoken to him personally, it doesn't matter—he is still insecure.

Fear is the antagonist of greatness! Fear takes us places we never imagined we'd go. Often due to our insecurities, fear will grip and sometimes cripple us from moving forward. Exodus 4:10-16 (NLT) highlights Moses' discussion with God about his fear:

But Moses pleaded with the Lord, "O Lord, I'm not very good with words. I never have been, and I'm not now, even though you have spoken to me. I get tongue-tied, and my words get tangled." Then the Lord asked Moses, "Who makes a person's mouth? Who decides whether people speak or do not speak, hear or do not hear, see or do not see? Is it not I, the lord? Now go! I will be with you as you speak, and I will instruct you in what to say." But Moses again pleaded, "Lord, please! Send anyone else." Then the Lord became angry with Moses. "All right," he said. "What about your brother, Aaron the Levite? I know he speaks well. And look! He is on his way to meet you now. He will be delighted to see you. Talk to him, and put the words in his mouth. I will be with both of you as you speak, and I will instruct you both in what to do. Aaron will be your spokesman to the people. He will be your mouthpiece, and you will stand in the place of God for him, telling him what to say.

Imagine God saying you are capable of doing something, but you're still paralyzed by fear! Fear is often rooted in our insecurity. In assessing your fears, consider these tips:

- Search your soul. Where is the fear coming from? Is it legitimate or are you simply not prepared?

- Trust God. When we are in His will, we have nothing to fear.

- If God has told us to do something and we refuse, we are being disobedient.

- There are consequences to inaction due to fear.

- God loves when His children trust Him and move forward in spite of fear.

What Are You Fearful Of?	How Can You Overcome Your Fear?

Closely related to fear is anxiety, a distress or uneasiness of mind caused by fear of danger or misfortune. The first time I had an anxiety attack, I didn't know that's what it was. I was overtaken by a sudden sense of fear from an inordinate amount of stress brought on by an overwhelming schedule and mounting task list. With the anxiety attack I had no control of my body. I had uncontrollable heavy breathing, sweaty palms, increased heart rate, and dizziness. Lack of control and dread plagued me. All sides were closing in around me and I had no way out. I wasn't very strong in my relationship with God at that time, but luckily a young lady, the "office pharmacist," had just what I needed...Xanax. Normally, I would never take medicine from someone who needed a daily dose of Percocet, Xanax, Valium, and Vicodin to get them through the day, but the thought of passing out in my client's office was not an option for my "in control" persona. Today, instead of the "office pharmacist," I use scriptures like the following to remedy anxiety:

- Proverbs 12:25 (NIV): "An anxious heart weighs a man down, but a kind word cheers him up."

- 1 Peter 5:7 (NIV): "Turn all your anxiety over to God because he cares for you."

- Jeremiah 17:7-8 (NIV): "But blessed is the man who trusts in the Lord, whose confidence is in him. He will be like a tree planted by the water that sends out its roots by the stream. It does not fear when heat comes; its leaves are always green. It has no worries in a year of drought and never fails to bear fruit."

I love this last scripture because it gives the benefits of trusting God: confidence and growth.

Besides fear, a lack of personal awareness is a critical greatness grabber.

Lack of Personal Awareness

When I was in Weight Watchers, they recommended that attendees know their trigger foods. Trigger foods were foods that at any moment might take you down the slippery slope and from size 6 back to size 16. My trigger foods are sweets. As a result, I plan accordingly. I avoid the dessert section at the buffet and don't purchase sweets at the grocery store. Knowing my trigger foods is key to reaching my goals. The same is true for personal awareness and who God says I am.

Psalm 139:14 (KJV) says, "I will praise thee; for I am fearfully and wonderfully made: marvelous are thy works; and that my soul knoweth right well." God knows us completely. We should get to know ourselves as intimately as God does. God celebrates our originality and personal diversity from anyone else, and so should we. My goal in life is to know myself fully. We should know ourselves more completely than anyone else does. **No one should ever tell you something you don't already know about yourself. The better I know myself, the easier it is for me to manage my emotions when dealing with others.**

Often after Spiritually Speaking programs, people invite me to lunch or dinner. I love spending time with people and was honored when dynamic women and men chose to spend their time with me. In reality, though, how could I ever get anything done if I entertained every invitation? To date, one of the greatest lessons I've learned is that I can be personable without becoming best friends with everyone. By including people in my existing schedule—gym, church, lunch hour, beauty appointments—I stick to my schedule *and* make time for others. This enables me to still engage people without overburdening my schedule. Without knowing myself and my limitations, I wouldn't have been able to make this adjustment.

Following my examples below, please write a couple of things you know about yourself that limit you in your business and personal life.

Things I know.	How this limits me.	How can I make this work in my favor?
I like sweets	*More pounds that I don't want*	*Ask friends to help me.*
I like to socialize	*Unnecessary time socializing*	*Include them in my regularly scheduled activities.*

Lack of Clear Expectations

Another greatness grabber is the lack of clear expectations. As an entrepreneur and a ministry leader, I often find myself doing something I never intended to do. For example, I'll volunteer to help with a task and end up doing most of the work. I'll say I can pick up my friend's child from the babysitter and she says, "Can she stay with you tonight?" Ordering flowers for the baby shower morphs into doing twenty things for a friend of a friend I only met two months ago. "Can you drop me off at the airport?" becomes the airport, bank, and three additional stops. I end up stressed and frustrated, all the time asking the question, "How did I get here?"

Too often, we allow the tides of other people's lives to drift us to places we never intended to go. As a marketing consultant, I work with many organizations and their boards. It rarely fails: there is usually a new person with wonderful ideas and fresh energy. They start spitting out ideas—good ones too—and everyone in the room is co-signing and on board—"Yeah, yeah, yeah, we should do that!" Then the moment arrives and it's time for action and the newbie is ready to work; unfortunately, they assume everyone else is too. But board obligations, schedules, meetings, vacations, kids, work, and life responsibilities slowly quench the fire everyone else had. Fast-forward one year and there's a new newbie and the process starts all over again. This used to happen to me quite often until I established clear expectations.

Establishing clear expectations isn't as easy as many think. It requires personal *self*-clarity. Self-clarity is knowing what we want and who we are. Without self-clarity, it's difficult to set expectations because we don't know who we are and what we require of ourselves. We certainly can't tell someone else what we require if we don't know what we require of ourselves, our wants, and our needs. **In order to set expectations, you must understand that everything is a transaction, an exchange of one thing for another.** Marriage is a transaction, friendship is a transaction, work is a transaction—everything is a transaction. We transact by exchanging one set of needs for another. Never enter any relationship without assessing these questions: *What does this person require? What do I need from this relationship? Are we compatible in our ideas, motives, intentions, capability, and capacity?*

In business, before starting a project, I meet with clients, assess their needs, and give them a verbal estimate based on our conversation. Within seven days, I forward clients a "Scope of Work" document that outlines specifically what I plan to offer and how much it's going to cost. I tell them exactly what services they can expect from me and what they may not expect from me. This removes the guess work and prevents many disagreements and misunderstandings.

Expectations and boundaries are completely different. **Expectations set the bar, whereas boundaries set the parameters—how high, how low, how right, or how left.** Boundaries are the longitude and latitude lines on a map; the expectation is the destination. If I enter a business relationship and tell my client that I will work on their project for ten hours a month, that's an expectation. Now, my boundary may be that I will not put in the ten hours unless they pay me in advance. They can expect me to do the work, but not outside the boundaries of the relationship. When expectations and boundaries are not established, parties end up frustrated and unclear about the relationship, whether business or personal.

In examining expectations, know whether the expectation is implied or set. An implied expectation is assumed and understood, and doesn't have to be stated. A set expectation is stated and/or written. For example, an implied expectation is that a spouse will not be unfaithful. A set expectation is that he or she will not have after-hour cocktails with the opposite sex. It's not elementary to write down your expectations before articulating them to someone else. When setting your expectations, never set an expectation that you yourself can't maintain—that's hypocritical.

Use the worksheet that follows to establish personal expectations.

Spiritual Expectations	Relationship Expectations	Career Expectations
I will give 10% of my income to the church and/or charity. I <u>expect</u> that if I sow bountifully, I will reap appropriately.	*I will put greater effort into my friendships. I <u>expect</u> my friends to contribute 50/50 to our relationships.*	*I will provide excellent client services. I <u>expect</u> to be compensated $195 per hour for my expertise and education.*

The Past

Our past can be the demon of our destiny if it's not in its proper place. **When we apprehend the past, we arrest our past sins and our past circumstances and take them into custody under our future prosperity. Allowing the past to linger undermines our future.** The Bible says we are cleansed from past sins. So if you slept with twenty or 200 men or women or both, had four abortions, lied, stole, robbed, or whatever, but confessed to God, He has forgiven you, and it's time for you to move to greatness. Past sin is obsolete…gone! Unfortunately, our feelings and failures still linger. But if the past contradicts our future, it must go. You can't aspire to be a physician while listening to the demons of your alcoholic father saying you'll never amount to anything. **You have to choose—stay still or move forward. You must decide today.**

Today, by most people's standards, I am successful. Yet I discovered I had not released all of my past circumstances. I am the child of a single mother who worked extremely hard to provide the best with limited resources. What we lacked in money, she made up in love. I remember being a cheerleader in junior high school. We had a weekend parade and had to wear new white Keds sneakers, but I knew my mother didn't have the money. It was either buy a new pair of Keds or eat. My mother decided that if she couldn't buy new sneakers, she would bleach the old ones I had. Well, too much bleach can put a hole in anything. Sure enough, that's what happened—a huge hole. So not only did I not have new Keds, but the old ones had a huge hole in the toe!

I tell that story because a few years ago I stood in front of more than 200 women at my Spiritually Speaking conference and told that story and began to weep hysterically. I was that little girl all over again. My past was the little girl who wasn't good enough, from the inner city, with the single-parent mother who was unable to defeat poverty. My present, as I stood at the front of that beautiful conference room, was that I still struggled with insecurity, self-doubt, and the residue of poverty, the result of an absent father and circumstances dictated by income. Life had dealt me a horrible hand, and at that moment I felt like I was never going to make it out. My past visited me that day, and even the fact that I was standing in front of that room looking beautiful and flawless didn't matter; I was still that little girl all over again.

Later I realized that even my weeping over my past was part of God's plan. I realized that my praying mother and God's hand had brought me to that Spiritually Speaking conference so those women could see my transparency, humility, and hope. God showed me how far he'd brought me from my past. In the past my mother didn't have enough money to buy me a new pair of Keds, but that day at that conference I could write a check for $10,000.

We must confront the past, embrace it, and remake it for our destiny. It's possible to move beyond the past and focus on who we are today. You can't look back and look forward at the same time.

What are some benchmarks or turning points in your past that may be limiting your destiny? Write them below.

Age	Benchmark/turning point	Have I healed from this? If not, how can I move on? (Talk to someone, ask God's forgiveness, forgive myself, etc.)
Before 12		
Teen years		
20s		

30s		
40s		
Recent		

Other People's Opinions

Another greatness grabber is other people's opinions. When we allow others to dictate our lives, it's difficult to move past our insecurities. We must assess our value independent of the thoughts, feelings, and opinions of others. Valuable people don't need other people's validation. We are God's creation; that's all the validation we need. "Am I now trying to win the approval of people or of God? If I were still trying to please people, I would not be the Messiah's servant." (Galatians 1:10, KJV).

One of my best friends became pregnant at age 15. At the time, she was one of the smartest students in her class, yet her favorite Latin teacher told her she wouldn't amount to anything because of her pregnancy . I'm pleased to say she now earns a six-figure income. Fortunately, she didn't heed the words of that teacher.

People can't make you more or less valuable, but we often do allow their expectations and opinions to tear us down or build us up. For that reason, we should surround ourselves with people who encourage us. Do your friends and associates expect the best from you? Do they validate and value you? I think great people always have cheerleaders to help them accomplish their greatness.

Our Imperfections

Do you know your blind spots and imperfections? In Jeremiah 18, God directed Jeremiah to go down to the potter's house and watch him molding clay into pots on his wheel. As Jeremiah watched, the potter discovered a flaw in the pot he was shaping. The potter pressed the clay into a lump and formed it into another pot. God announced to Jeremiah that the potter and the clay illustrated His relationship with His people. They are like clay in His hand, and He has the right to tear down or build up a nation as He pleases. God specializes in transforming marred vessels. If we learn nothing else from this passage, we know that God made us and God can remake us. Countless people in the Bible were flawed, but God remade and redirected their lives. Here are just a few:

- Rahab the prostitute saved Joshua's spies and went on to be the mother of Boaz in the line of Christ. Christ's lineage was full of undesirables by today's standards.

- Manasseh, King of Judah, shed innocent blood, but repented and was restored to his kingdom.

- David sinned with Bathsheba, but repented and went on to rule over all twelve tribes of Judah and to be one of Israel's greatest kings.

- Paul persecuted Christians, but later became instrumental in founding the Christian movement.

In my own life when I had been fornicating all over the country, God remade me. First, God showed me my value. When we know our value in God, others see it too. Second, I began to hold a greater standard for myself. When you value yourself, you set a higher premium on everything you do, not just relationships. Last, I learned to value purpose, not position. Sure, I worked at Black Entertainment Television (BET); that was fun, but that was not what gave me value. My value was in my destiny; BET was simply a stop along the way.

I needed a spiritual makeover. It was a makeover money couldn't buy, no man could fill, and drugs and alcohol couldn't satisfy...only Christ could! I learned my purpose and calling—to help believers walk in God's fullness and to live a more Christ-like life.

Romans 9:21 (NIV): "Does not the potter have the right to make out of the same lamp of clay some pottery for noble purposes and some for common use?"

When looking at your imperfections, ask yourself the following questions:

- Am I a marred vessel?
- Can I be repaired?
- Am I living up to Christ's expectations?

The answer to the first two questions is yes. We are all marred in some way, and Christ can repair us. The answer to the third question is up to you. Sometimes it helps to see what God has already done for us. Use the table below to document five previous imperfections and how God has made them over. Share your testimony of at least one of these incidents with someone this week. For #6, write an imperfection you are currently dealing with. How might God do a spiritual makeover in this area?

Imperfection	How and when God did a spiritual makeover
1.	
2.	
3.	
4.	
5.	
6. Current	

Lack of Follow-Through

Lack of follow-through is another greatness grabber. I used to start projects and never complete them. I would get frustrated with myself or with other people and quit. Starting your own business will certainly put the kibosh on your lack of follow-through—that is, if you want the business to be successful. If you don't work, you don't eat. A place where this lack of follow-through still influences me is dieting. I start the diet, see results, get bored or distracted, have a cupcake, and swell up again.

I see our youth in a similar, yet even more destructive, pattern in the ferocious cycle of the revolving criminal justice system. They start off on the right track with big plans and high hopes, only to be seduced back into their life of crime. While incarcerated, they cite all the wonderful things they're going to do and how they're going to get their life together. For the most part, their emotions and sentiments are genuine…they really believe what they're saying. But then they return home…free to go through the same revolving door yet again. Proverbs 26:11 (NIV) says, "As a dog returns to its vomit, so a fool repeats his folly."

Perhaps we don't know any other way, so we keep doing the same thing. But insanity has been defined as doing the same thing over and over and expecting different results. Our lack of follow-through could be a sign of sloth. Whatever the cause—boredom, distractions, sloth, fear, or lack of discipline—not finishing becomes a lifelong pattern. We never finish our commitments to our destiny, to others, or to self.

As an entrepreneur, I have a diverse group of clients, from sole proprietorships to corporations worth $90 billion. When I initially started consulting, I didn't want to work with difficult clients. I would either not follow through or refund their money. As I matured professionally and spiritually, I learned to identify clients' personalities early on. Now I might refer the project to someone else or add an additional surcharge to make it worth my while. Listening teaches you the warning signs for challenging clients. Experience teaches you how to keep the peace. My reputation and business are successful as a result of my follow-through. The personal benefits are evident as well: financial gain, access to greater opportunities, and more patience. My best projects have been those where I had little to no initial interest, yet which brought big rewards, such as worldwide access, business opportunities, and new relationships.

Take the time to examine some unfinished business and make a plan to follow it to completion:

List unfinished projects	Develop plan (with timeline) to follow through
Finish my book.	*Write one chapter a month so book will be finished in a year.*

Lack of Focus

There is a quote by Jim Rohn that says, "What we ponder and what we think about sets the course of our life." Nothing is achieved without focus. There are many things that rob our greatness, but few like lack of focus. In my lifetime, I've seen people run the treadmill of events, activities, and projects and never arrive at their destination—greatness. Our success directly correlates to how well we FOCUS. I use this acronym to define focus: **Finding Our**

Challenges that **U**ndermine **S**uccess. Many believe focus is simply striving for a destination. Focus is also removing the things that hinder us from arriving at our destination, trimming the fat. I had to move to London to finally complete *Chasing Greatness*. There were simply too many distractions in the States. Challenges might include people who take up too much time, things that compromise our productivity, and places that hinder our progress. This arrow demonstrates the process for achieving goals.

Write all the people, places, and things that hinder your focus and your plan to get back on track:

People, places, and things that hinder my focus	Plan to get back on track
Talking on the telephone when I should be working.	*Turn the ringer off, reward myself with a phone call to a friend once my work is done.*

Many of the strategies I have applied in my own life and in business have been a result of the principles in the Bible. No other story in the Bible resonates like 2 Kings 18. King Hezekiah was the fourteenth King of Judah and came to the throne at age 25. He is described as an able and pious ruler. He carefully worked to free Judah from Assyrian political and religious domination. During his reign he not only eliminated idols, divination practices, and human sacrifices, but he also did away with cult objects and pagan practices. King Hezekiah demonstrated successful leadership in five stages:

#1 Destroying the old things that keep or hold us back from God. "He removed the pagan shrines, smashed the sacred pillars and knocked down the Asherah poles. He broke up the bronze serpent that Moses had made, because the people of Israel had begun to worship it by burning incense to it" (verse 4, NLT). We must clean our slate and remove things that hinder our spiritual growth.

#2 Trusting the Lord and putting our confidence in Him. "Hezekiah trusted in the LORD, the God of Israel. There was no one like him among all the kings of Judah, either before him or after him" (verse 5, NLT). Trust means to put one's confidence in, to hope for. Not trust in ourselves, but trust in God, even when it doesn't make sense. There is a difference between believing God will deliver and *knowing* God will deliver. We need to move from a believing faith to a knowing faith. With believing you may doubt, but with knowing you are certain.

#3 Holding fast to our faith in the Lord. "He remained faithful to the LORD in everything" (verse 6a, NLT). Without faith it really is impossible to please God. We need faith for God to act. I can desire, but faith is the knowing, the certainty that God will perform. People with small faith doubt, but big faith moves God to action.

#4 Obeying God's commandments carefully. "...And he carefully obeyed all the commands the LORD had given Moses" (verse 6b, NLT). There was conscientiousness with his actions. When you carefully obey, a greater level of consideration and care goes into your actions. You are concerned about the outcome as well.

#5 Relationship. "So the LORD was with him, and Hezekiah was successful in everything he did... He also conquered the Philistines as far distant as Gaza and its territory, from their smallest outpost to their largest walled city (verses 7-8, NLT)." The only other time the Bible says, "the LORD was with him," is in reference to King David. Greater protection, provision, and production come when the Lord is with us.

Greatness grabbers come in many forms. We need to be more than just aware of things that prevent greatness; we need to be armed so we won't succumb to their temptations. Anything from sin to fear, to other people, to lack of direction can steal greatness from us. Be aware and be armed. If we don't believe our own greatness, no one else will. Chapter 5 looks further into thinking and believing greatness.

Chapter Highlights

- Fear is the antagonist of greatness. Fear takes us places we never imagined we'd go. Often due to our insecurities, fear will grip and sometimes cripple us from moving forward.

- When you possess personal awareness, you know more about yourself than someone else knows about you. No one should ever tell you something you don't know about yourself. We should know ourselves as intimately as God does.

- Self-clarity is knowing what we want and who we are.

- In order to set expectations, you must understand that everything is a transaction, an exchange of one thing for another, especially relationships.

- Expectations set the bar, whereas boundaries set the parameters—how high, how low, how right, or how left.

- An implied expectation is assumed and understood and doesn't have to be stated. A set expectation is stated and/or written.

- When we apprehend the past, we take our past sins and circumstances into custody and arrest them under our future prosperity. Allowing the past to linger undermines our future.

- When we allow others to dictate our lives, it's difficult to move past our own insecurities. We must assess our value independent of the thoughts, feelings, and opinions of others.

- When you value yourself, you set a higher premium on your goods in everything you do—not just in relationships. Learn to value purpose, not position.

- Our lack of follow-through may be a sign of sloth.

- Focus is *removing* the things that hinder us from arriving at our destination. Our success directly correlates to how well we FOCUS: Finding Our Challenges that Undermine Success.

Up Next ⇨

Thinking and Believing Greatness alerts us to mental skills that will assist us in achieving greatness, including learning to listen, seeing ourselves realistically, reshaping our thinking, understanding God's purpose for us, detoxing from bitterness, and creating personal intimacy.

CHAPTER 5

Thinking and Believing Greatness

CHAPTER 5
Thinking and Believing Greatness

It's a funny thing about life; if you refuse to accept anything but the best, you very often get it.

—Somerset Maughan

Without the mind's active participation, we can never attain greatness. Unfortunately, many of us are defeated mentally before we take action physically. Proverbs 23:7 (KJV) says, "For as he thinketh in his heart, so is he." If I believe I am nothing, that's what I become and that is how people will treat me. Remember, the body cannot achieve what the mind cannot conceive. Decide, commit, and succeed in greatness.

The tools in this chapter have laid the foundation for my personal success in everything I do, and if you apply them, they can do the same for you.

Listen More, Speak Less

I meet many wealthy people and have noticed that a trait most common among them is silence. Let's be honest: there are a shortage of good listeners in our society. In listening more, you gain a greater appreciation of people. Listening cautiously is an advantage in building healthy, well-rounded, and authentic relationships. By super-sizing our listening skills, we contribute to the cultivation of strong relationships. Listen twice as much as you speak.

Attentive listening is not waiting for your turn to talk. It's hearing and comprehending who the person is and what they value. It allows you to gain a greater perspective. Inattentive listening is a symptom of pride. A surface conversation can only give you surface results. The assumption with inattentive listening is that I have something more important to say than the other person. When I put my ego to the side, am quiet, and listen, I walk away with a greater sense of a person's mission, goals, fears, and hopes—their total being.

Alter Your Expectations

Your thoughts are the architects of your destiny.

—David O. McKay

Greatness is a state of mind, not a permanent destination. If I don't know I'm great, then I will never act in my greatness. Notice I said *know*, and not *believe*. Remember, believing is external, but knowing is internal. When you know who you are, people can't shake you. **A person who only believes,**

thinks, *This could happen, maybe...* But a person who knows, says, *When this happens, I will...* The power is in the knowing, and the knowing brings the action.

In Numbers 13, the Lord asked Moses to send a man from each of the twelve tribes of Israel to search the land of Canaan, which God had provided for them. After forty days, the men returned from searching the land and gave an account to Moses and Aaron. Caleb reported that the people in the land were strong and the cities were walled and very great. He also insisted they go up at once and possess it. But the other eleven men who had gone with Caleb had a different perspective. They saw the same things visually, but they didn't want to fight for the land. They said of the people, "And there we saw the giants, the sons of Anak, which come of the giants: and we were in our own sight as grasshoppers, and so we were in their sight" (Numbers 13:33, NLT). One man saw a land to possess; the others thought of themselves as grasshoppers because they didn't have faith in themselves or in the greatness God had placed within them.

We need more "Caleb Confidence" in the world! Caleb said, "Let's go up at once, and take possession, for we are well able to overcome it" (Numbers 13:30, NKJV). Caleb was eager to possess his promise, his blessing. His statement showed urgency, ownership, and dominion. Notice, Caleb's mindset was what he *could do*, not what he *couldn't do*. In order for us to inhabit God's best, we must dwell in His promises for our lives. Faith is always supported by action. How can we not have faith when God has already told us to go and possess what's ours? Don't continue to dwell with less than God's standard when He's already given you ownership! Are you *God's* best or are you *man's* best? Anything less than God's best is average, and not greatness!

I admit I can be a little arrogant at times when it comes to my relationship with God. I have a spoiled-daughter complex and I don't expect God to say *no* to my requests. Yet when He does say *no* or *not now*, I rest in the fact that it's for my best interest, and not my flesh's interest.

Once I began to inhabit God's dwelling place, I couldn't go slumming anymore. It became a contradiction to who I am and what I know. The big difference between Caleb and the other guys whose names didn't make the Bible was that Caleb lived up to the legacy of his family, the Tribe of Judah—confident warriors. He possessed that confidence, that greatness. Yet, the others saw themselves as they thought the giants saw them. Never be concerned with how others see you.

There is a saying that *well-behaved women seldom make history*. I think about women like Rahab who risked her own life to help the Hebrew spies; or Queen Esther who breached protocol and went before King Xerxes when it was not customary to do so, in order to save her people; or Deborah, the first and only female judge of Israel. These women, like so many other women, are celebrated now, but during their time they were trendsetters for change and went against traditional culture. Their capacity to do so was rooted in the fact that they knew their own power. **As individuals, we must know our own power, before we can project our power onto someone else.** We cannot move forward in our greatness if we don't recognize the greatness within ourselves. **People who *don't* know their power *don't* get their names listed in books.** If I don't recognize myself as belonging to the Tribe of the King, I can never inhabit my greatness. You should *expect* others to say yes. You should expect nothing less than the best. You should expect opportunities. Yes, you should expect greatness. Altering expectations means reshaping thoughts.

Reshape Your Thinking

One cannot think crooked and walk straight.

—Anonymous

Can I believe in God and His promises yet not make the connection between possibility and promise? **Possibility says there *could be* something greater, but promise says there *is* something greater.** We need to move from a *defeated* mindset to a *dominion* mindset. Philippians 4:8 (KJV) says, "Finally, brethren, whatsoever things are true, whatsoever things are honest, whatsoever things are just, whatsoever things are pure, whatsoever things are lovely, whatsoever things are of good report; if there be any virtue, and if there be any praise, think on these things." A dominion mindset implies ownership, but defeat indicates subjection. Ephesians 3:20 (KJV) says, "Now unto him that is able to do exceeding abundantly above all that we ask or think, according to the power that worketh in us...."

The scriptures above are what I call contingency scriptures. They are based on something that we ourselves must personally do or internally possess. For example, we can receive all we ask—and more!—"according to the power that worketh in us." **Getting all we ask is contingent on the existing power actually working in our lives, now.** If I have no power, then how is anything going to work? Power is internal and starts simply with what we know, not what we believe. **Some of us will never be great because we haven't decided to activate our greatest asset: our mind.**

When I reflect on the powerful blessings of God, I think of Matthew 17:20, where Jesus tells the disciples that they failed in casting out a demon, "because you have so little faith. I tell you the truth: if you have faith as small as a mustard seed, you can say to this mountain, 'Move from here to there' and it will move. Nothing will be impossible for you" (NIV). As children, we didn't stress about where our meals came from; we just knew we would eat. We need to have that same childlike faith with Christ. Don't second-guess God's blessing for you; *know* He has blessing.

Purposed by God, Not by People

When you know who you are, you don't need validation from others. Jeremiah 1:5 (NLT) says, "I knew you before I formed you in your mother's womb. Before you were born I set you apart and appointed you as my prophet to the nations." Let's look at this scripture closely:

- **Before I formed you (Purposed).** We were birthed by God with intention, an anticipated outcome that we are expected to fulfill. Our actions should be made with this outcome in mind.

- **Before you were born (Positioned).** We have a place, a destiny that God has established for us. Every individual born into this world has a place that God has established for him or her. A job that no one but you can fill. Thus, a wayward life, one resistant to guidance and discipline, is not the life God intended for you.

- **I appointed you as a prophet (Promoted).** Born for greatness. God wants us to have a high place. When we think we can't lose or feel we are defeated, we should know that we were born to succeed no matter how bad the situation looks.

We must never give people who don't know us the power to render an opinion about our purpose that could leave us feeling flawed. If I saw you get into an argument with someone at the grocery store and saw you preaching the next day, would I have the right to make a final decision about your character from a fifteen-minute incident? More importantly, why do we allow people with such limited knowledge of our character to render an opinion about us, which we take to heart and embrace as our personal truth, thus allowing their opinions to shape how we see ourselves? Sure, it's important to be aware of our reputation but we will want to give much more credibility to those who know us best and who care about us sincerely enough to speak the truth in love (Ephesians 4:15). Of course, no one will ever know us as completely as God does.

In sharing our personal business, there are some discussions for you and God only, some discussions for you and wise counsel, and last, some discussions for your family. As demonstrated in the chart below, Jesus' life provided a great example of what portions of our business and private thoughts we should share with whom.

	With Whom To Share (Biblical Example)	With Whom To Share (Today)	What To Share
PERSONALLY	God	You and God only	Everything. Things that require clarity
PRIVATELY	James, John and Peter	Inner circle of 3 closest spiritually mature friends	Personal and intimate things that require counsel or confirmation

SELECTIVELY	12 Disciples	Family/ Friends	Personal successes that encourage others
PUBLICLY	Followers	All like-minded people	Things that promote God and not ourselves

Relationships are necessary for greatness. People in the inner circle should know our parameters, specifically what we value and what disgusts us. Awareness of and adherence to these parameters reveals their ability to respect our boundaries. Friendships with no boundaries are problematic. The most important relationship is, obviously, with God, but other people—supportive, loving, and respectful friends and family—also usher us into greatness.

Detox from Bitterness

For a brief time I lived with a woman whose husband had left her to be with his mistress. To add insult to injury, he excelled after he left. Her ex-husband moved on and seemed happy with a new baby, a thriving career, a fabulous house, and lots of money. In contrast, my landlord's life was miserable, and she made mine a living hell because of her bitterness. According to her, life was pretty terrific before she met him and he took everything she had. I sympathize with her situation. You put your all into a relationship only to be let down and left with nothing. Who wouldn't be angry? Yet being angry and harboring bitterness are two completely different things. Bitter people are so consumed with hate they can't move forward; they become poisoned by it. Bitter people will hurt themselves in order to get even or damage another. The best remedy for bitterness is God. We cannot move forward until we forgive and relinquish the situation to God.

Detoxification is removing everything that hinders our progress and keeps us from moving forward. It's really an amputation of sorts, removing a gangrenous limb. No one wants to look back and see all their time, resources, and energy put into a situation that leaves them bitter, lonely, and empty-handed. But you can't appreciate someone who treats you like gold, until you've had someone who treated you like crap. To name just one example, until you have a boss micromanage you, you can't appreciate someone who trusts and respects your talent.

Everyone gets taken, sometimes by those closest to them. **Fortunately, the lessons guide the way to your blessings.** We can't improve when we hold on to bitterness. Until you recover, you can't discover. Bitterness disables and binds us from moving forward. I say, learn the lesson, get the blessing, and **DIG *(Determine Inhibitions to Greatness)*. Discovering what went wrong is paramount to ensuring it won't happen again.**

Self Intimacy

The French author, Francois de La Rochefoucauld, said, "When a man finds no peace within himself, it is useless to seek it elsewhere...We are so accustomed to disguising ourselves to others, we become disguised to ourselves."

Do we really know who we are? Heck, no! We have become so accustomed to being with other people all the time that we've lost the ability to be comfortable alone; we've lost self intimacy. Developing personal intimacy requires spending time alone. In my early 20s, I would never go to a restaurant or a movie alone. Now I do it all the time. **Spending time alone enables me to process my thoughts, emotions, and feelings.** I'm surprised how many people can't be alone and just be quiet, with no television, radio, or other distractions.

I see this fear of being alone in dating relationships. Some will go to any length to avoid being alone. No sooner is girlfriend A on her way out than girlfriend B is prospected and friend C is benched for potential girlfriend rotation. Yes, women do it too. The problem with this is that the man (or woman) is never alone. He doesn't take time to discover what he truly wants and needs in a relationship because he doesn't know who he is.

It took me a while but after spending time with myself, my values and personality were nothing like I first thought they were. Self-discovery revealed who I was and what I needed. In the interest of doing some self-discovery of your own, examine your life and complete each sentence below:

I find it difficult to <u>listen</u> when _____

_____

I need to alter the following <u>self-perceptions:</u> _____

_____

I want to <u>reshape my thinking</u> by_____

_____

I can rely on these people in my <u>inner circle</u> to influence me positively: ___

_____

I still hold <u>bitterness</u> in this area: _____

_____

I've mistakenly allowed this one moment to <u>define</u> my life: _____

_____

I will spend time <u>alone</u> by _____

_____

Chapter Highlights

- Active listening is not waiting for your turn to talk. It's actually hearing and comprehending who the other person is and what they value.

- Inactive listening is a symptom of pride.

- When I put my ego to the side, am quiet, and listen, I walk away with a greater sense of a person's mission, goals, fears and hopes— their total being.

- Greatness is a state of mind, not a permanent destination.

- A person who only believes, thinks, *This could happen, maybe....* But a person who knows, says, *When this happens, I will....* The power is in the knowing, and the knowing brings the action.

- Possibility says there *could be* something greater, but promise says there *is* something greater.

- As individuals we must know our own power in order to project our power onto someone else.

- People who don't know their power don't get their names listed in history books.

- Getting all we ask is contingent on the existing power actually working in our lives, now.

- When you know who you are, you don't need validation from others. Never give people who don't know you the power to render an opinion that leaves you feeling flawed.

- Some of us will never be great until we activate our greatest asset: our mind.

- Detoxification is removing everything that hinders our progress and keeps us from moving forward.

- In sharing our personal business, there are some discussions for us and God, some discussions for us and our wise counsel, and some discussions for our family.

- When learning life lessons, we must DIG—**D**etermine **I**nhibitions to **G**reatness.

- Developing personal intimacy requires spending time alone. Spending time alone enables us to process our thoughts, emotions, and feelings.

Up Next ⇨

Acting in Greatness explores how knowing the truth and acting on it are two different things. We'll look at the evolution of greatness and key ways to act in greatness with an emphasis on finding mentors and setting goals.

Acting in Greatness

CHAPTER 6
Acting in Greatness

Are you fit company for the person you wish to become?

—Anonymous

I spent so many years moving in the wrong direction...spinning my bicycle spokes when I should have put my kickstand down on a completely different road. I acted in desperation. I acted in the flesh. I acted in anger. But today I'm proud to say most of my actions are in greatness. The process might be simpler to explain by using the apostle Paul as an example of what it means to act in greatness. Let's look at Acts 9 to reflect on the process of conversion for Paul (who was also called Saul):

- **THE CALL:** "And he fell to the earth, and heard a voice saying unto him, Saul, Saul, why persecutest thou me?" (Acts 9:4, KJV). I'm sure Paul had no idea why he fell to the ground that day, but God knew. The very God he had persecuted for years became the same God he unconsciously surrendered to. **Oftentimes, we unconsciously accept God's call before we consciously accept His direction.**

- **DIRECTION AND DUTY:** "And he trembling and astonished said, Lord, what wilt thou have me to do? And the Lord said unto him, Arise, and go into the city, and it shall be told thee what thou must do" (Acts 9:6, KJV). God always has a direction, even if we don't yet have His marching orders. Paul engaged God by asking, "Lord, what wilt thou have me to do?" Actively participating in God's direction gives us a greater sense of fulfillment. It wasn't until I started living God's plan for my life that I felt alive. Sure, before then I was living life, but I wasn't truly *alive*. I just existed in the day-to-day.

- **OBEDIENCE:** "Saul got up from the ground, and though his eyes were open, he could see nothing; and leading him by the hand, they brought him into Damascus" (Acts 9:8, NASB). It is one thing to get God's direction, but it's another to be obedient. To paraphrase John 14:15, if we love God, we will keep His commandments.

- **TOOLS OF GOD:** "But the Lord said to [Ananias], Go, for he is a chosen instrument of Mine, to bear My name before the Gentiles and kings and the sons of Israel; for I will show him how much he must suffer for My name's sake" (Acts 9:15-16, NASB). We are tools for manifesting God's greatness on earth. People should see God in our lives. Our bodies should symbolize God's best; our actions and speech should be examples for others to follow. Everything about us should epitomize God on earth. **Our duty is to represent God in a way that entices people to desire God in a more intimate way.** When people ask, *Why are you so different?* that's when you know you're doing something right.

- **PREPARATION:** "And he took food and was strengthened. Now for several days he was with the disciples who were at Damascus" (Acts 9:19, NASB). Have you noticed that success is often directly tied to preparation? What we learn during the preparation time is the foundation for the elevation. **The amount of preparation time is directly related to our elevation altitude.**

- **TIMING:** "And immediately he began to proclaim Jesus in the synagogues, saying, He is the Son of God" (Acts 9:20). Sometimes God says, *Go immediately.* More often, at least in my life, he says, *Wait.* **God's perfect timing is the moment when opportunity and destiny collide.**

- **PRACTICE:** "And immediately he began to proclaim Jesus in the synagogues, saying, He is the Son of God" (Acts 9:20, NASB). **In our time of preparation we must practice the traits needed for our destiny.** If God called me to be a business owner, I'd practice negotiation. If He called me to be an evangelist, I'd practice speaking. If He called me to be a wife and mother, I'd practice the skills necessary to fulfill those roles well. Practice how you're going to participate and compete in your industry. Practice, practice, practice.

- **PERFECTION, PROCLAMATION, AND RESULT:** "But Saul kept increasing in strength and confounding the Jews who lived at Damascus by proving that this Jesus is the Christ" (Acts 9:22, NASB). I love this scripture because it outlines how Paul continued to evolve. Our spiritual journey is ever evolving. When I survey each year of my life, I want to see improvements over the prior year. What improvements have you made from year to year?

Today (*How did your life improve from last year?*)_____

_____

Last year (*How did your life improve from two years ago?*) _____

_____

2 years ago (*How did your life improve from three years ago?*) _____

_____

3 years ago (*How did your life improve from four years ago?*) _____

_____

4 years ago (*How did your life improve from five years ago?*) _____

_____

Greatness isn't a spectator sport; it requires active participation. We must *act* to secure greatness. I can no more attain greatness being a spectator than I can obtain six-pack abs by watching television. We've seen Paul's process; here are some additional keys to acting in greatness. The best place to begin is with an attitude of excellence.

Develop Excellence

Mediocrity is excellence to the eyes of mediocre people.

—Joseph Joubert

As an entrepreneur and a Christian, a big challenge for me is helping others move from mediocrity to excellence. **As we move from mediocrity, there are three things that can never be challenged: *education, experience,* and *excellence*—what I'd like to call a triple threat or the 3 Es.** Education (our preparation), excellence (our presentation), and experience (our participation) align to optimize our greatness. Success is measured by one or all three of the above—what you have done, what you have learned, or what you have perfected.

To operate at the maximum level of excellence, we must think big-picture, not small-frame. We must move past ourselves to achieve excellence and not embrace the mentality of *this is the way it's always been done.* Early in my career, I couldn't tell you what to listen for to determine a person's level of excellence or lack thereof. Now, I listen for disclaimers about why they *can't* do something. I look for former corporate superstars who now operate at C level—just average. Excellence isn't average. By definition, it is always A-level.

When sustaining your A game, performance is a critical component. That means performing above and beyond what is needed or expected. It's giving the extra 50% necessary to operate above the rest. I hope others will see my performance and become better themselves because of my example. Raising my own bar breeds consistency and responsibility in those around me.

Operating at an A level in a C-level environment can be inhibited by three key things: *time, knowledge,* and *staff.* Lack of time management robs us of proper planning and often causes us to be hurried and not put our best foot forward. For obvious reasons, a lack of knowledge directly robs us of our A game. We should be in a constant state of learning. And sometimes uncommitted staff members can undermine your Level A. Such may be especially true when working in ministry since most ministries are volunteer-based.

To maximize staff contributions, it's essential to have people operating in their **sweet spot, where their passion meets their purpose.** The biggest indicator of someone *not* operating in their sweet spot is confusion and disorder, but a great leader won't cast them out. A great leader will build them up and find the right place for them. Operating at A level means engaging the right staff—an employee, volunteer, friend, even co-worker—and figuring out what excites them, not who can simply do the job. Even Jesus paid attention and took the time and care necessary to develop each disciple. For volunteers it could be by trial and error; for a friend it could be selecting activities that take them out of their comfort zone; for an employee or co-worker it could be helping them identify corporate projects that excite them.

In ministry, I pride myself on producing quality programs that represent Christ. In business, I give my clients the best service available. "Average" is a waste of time for me. I'm only concerned with excellence. **Excellence attracts excellence.** This means carefully examining my friends and peers. If most of the people I know are average, then I probably am too; if they are moving toward greatness, then so am I. **If they are in the same place today that they were in last year, so am I.** I should ensure friends are pursuing the same level of excellence and greatness as I am. When I determine my level of excellence, the least I can do is help a friend by encouraging theirs.

Ignore Naysayers

Even those with a track record of success encounter naysayers. If we don't have people who envy us, we're probably not on our way to greatness. Envy appears at every level of personal promotion. As I started to advance, I couldn't understand why all people just didn't love me. Eventually, I figured out that to stress about why others don't like me is crazier than them not liking me!

On the flip-side, when *I* compare myself to others, *I* am in danger of becoming envious. Comparing leads to envy and jealousy, and ultimately undermines my own greatness. I can compliment others without comparing: "I really admire that about her…; I respect how he does…; and she's really good at that."

My former landlord told me that I made her feel inadequate and inferior. First, I can never make someone feel anything unless they allow me to. **Inferiority develops from low self-esteem.** God's light in me causes people to see things about themselves, but God's light never brings malicious intent. I didn't waste time defending myself and I certainly didn't expend too much emotional or spiritual time with her inadequacies. Take mental inventory to see if you need to approach someone differently in the future. Other than that, naysayers have no place in my greatness, or yours. I think the quote by Fulton J. Sheen says it best: "Jealousy is the tribute mediocrity pays to genius."

Find Mentors

Elisha had Elijah, Timothy had Paul, and Joshua had Moses. The Bible is full of outstanding mentoring relationships. These relationships represent a changing of the guard, where mentors pass the baton and the mentee goes further than the mentor. Mentors are a key ingredient to developing great-ness. **Great mentors open doors, create opportunities, and secure resources on behalf of their mentee.** The mentor nurtures dynamic and fresh talent for greatness when the mentee demonstrates the potential necessary for that relationship.

Dictionary.com defines a mentor as an influential senior sponsor or supporter. I love that word *sponsor* because a sponsor vouches for and is responsible for the other person. A great mentor is responsible for the mentee emotionally, intellectually, socially, and fiscally.

A mentor is emotionally responsible because they guide the mentee regard-ing how and what to communicate. A mentor is intellectually responsible because they lead the mentee professionally in their trade or industry, and is socially responsible, introducing the mentee to new social circles and provid-ing access for opportunities. Lastly, a mentor should be fiscally responsible by economically empowering the mentee, not necessarily by giving them money, but by enhancing their opportunities for economic success.

Mentoring is a huge responsibility that requires hard work and commitment. It's a long-term, intensive relationship, not a quarterly dinner or lunch engage-ment. The mentee becomes the mentor's shadow, an extension of themselves. The mentor's life has to be in order before they can competently mentor someone else. How can I be a realtor and not own a home? How can I mentor married couples if my marriage is in shambles?

Now that we have developed excellence, built a reputation, ignored the naysayers, and found an appropriate mentor, it's time to develop our strat-egy for action.

A Plan of Action

That first peak is the best place to pause and look back, to see if you took the easiest route, to learn the lessons from the first climb. And it is the best place to examine the terrain ahead, to change your plans and goals, to take a deep breath and begin climbing again.

—Michael Johnson

A strategy is more important than even a compass. A compass is a tool, but a strategy is a plan for using the tool. Having money without a plan is like walking around with a hole in your pocket. In your honest opinion, can you successfully answer the following questions?

- *Are you where you want to be?* I meet people who go to law school. Years later (after accumulating massive student loans), they open a flower shop. I know a man who went to medical school because his parents insisted on it, but his dream was to work as a musician. It's not enough to know that where you are is not where you want to be. You have to make the effort to change your destination.

- *Where do you want to be?* Every great journey starts with a destination, a direction. Ask yourself probing questions: Ten years from now, where and who do I want to be? What do I want the content of my character to be? For years, I was a solo entrepreneur. When I took a step back, I realized I didn't necessarily want a marketing company; I just wanted a decent income. I didn't want a multi-level conglomerate; I just wanted a vacation home, a nice car, and the opportunity to do what fulfilled me. Years later I refocused. I decided what I wanted was a simpler, low-maintenance business with a decent income. That's what I have today. Shifting not only changes your direction; it changes your destiny.

- *Are my goals realistic?* I want to be the next American Idol. I want my book on Oprah. I want a million dollars by the end of the year. Well, if I can't sing, haven't written a word, and am a million dollars in debt, these goals probably aren't very realistic. When setting goals, be adventurous and willing to take risks, but not outrageous. To rethink those goals, I say: I want to take singing lessons, finish my book, and put $1,000 a month toward my debt. Okay, now we're entering into the reality zone. Dream big, but not so big that those dreams are unachievable.

- *Have I set timeframes for my goals?* All well-thought-out objectives have a timeframe. What's your timeframe to lose ten pounds? What's your timeframe to get a new house? What's your timeframe to get a new job? What's your timeframe for completing college? **Timeframes help us identify where we are and where we should be and by when.** For example, if you've set a timeframe for completing school within six years but now it's year eight, that is cause to ring the alarm. Attach a timeframe to every objective you set. Monitor and readjust timeframes as necessary.

- *What's my recovery strategy?* Aldous Huxley said, "Experience is not what happens to a man; it's what a man does with what happens to him." Sometimes circumstances and relationships don't work out the way we planned. **Rebounding is bouncing or springing back from a force of impact. Every goal and objective should have a recovery strategy.** Even as a Christian, sometimes I mistake *my* desire for God's will and miss the mark. So I ask myself, *What now? What's my Plan B?* Having a Plan B helps minimize the impact of a set-back just like a savings account minimizes the financial impact of losing your job. Usually, if I have to implement my Plan B, it was the Lord's Plan A anyway. A verse that helps my recovery strategy is Romans 8:28 (NIV): "And we know that in all things God works for the good of those who love him, who have been called according to his purpose." Use the chart below to set realistic goals with timeframes; anticipate potential obstacles and how you will recover from them.

Goal	Strategy	Timeframe	Plan B
Add six new clients	*Attend three networking events*	*Next 60 days*	*Send mailing to current customers asking for referrals*
		Next week	
		Next month	
		Next quarter	
		Next year	
		Next three years	
		Next five years	

- *Do I have relationships with people who create new opportunities for me?* In business, it's important to meet new people who will introduce new interests and create new experiences. Think outside the box and meet new people who bring new opportunities for you.

- *Do I act great even when I don't feel great?* **God's goal is to get high-capacity activity out of low-capacity people; to move us from our human hierarchy to our heavenly highchair.** Unfortunately, sometimes we don't feel ready. So, we must learn to thrive even when we are uncomfortable—during frustrations, foreclosures, and other life flops. Pick up the attitude of the place you want to be and dwell there. Find the feeling and embrace it; occupy the space even when you don't feel like it.

Act as if greatness has already been achieved. Dress like the stylist you will one day be. If you want to be a teacher, teach in your daily interactions. If you want to be an actor, perform in a community theater production.

When I wanted to expand globally, I didn't buy *InStyle* magazine; I bought *The New Yorker*, *The Economist* and *The Standard*. I didn't listen to or watch MTV; I watched and listened to the BBC. Jesus started teaching when he was twelve. David killed Goliath before he inherited the throne, and Joseph embraced his dreams when he was a boy. Walk in your dream.

Acting in Greatness—A Step of Faith

This chapter has provided all the tools for you to act in greatness. Show me a person who isn't doing this and I'll show you a person who lacks the faith necessary to get it done. A person of faith walks differently than someone without faith. I quoted Matthew 17:20 earlier, but it seems fitting to repeat it: "For verily I say unto you, If ye have faith as a grain of mustard seed, ye shall say unto this mountain, Remove hence to yonder place; and it shall remove; and nothing shall be impossible unto you" (KJV). It's time to act in greatness!

Chapter Highlights

- The process of greatness includes: *the call, direction and duty, obedience, tools of God, preparation, timing, practice, perfection, proclamation,* and *results.*

- There are three things about greatness that can never be challenged: *education, experience,* and *excellence.*

- Education (our preparation), excellence (our presentation), and experience (our participation) align to optimize our greatness.

- Success is measured by one or all three of the above, which may also be phrased: *what you have done, what you have learned,* and *what you have perfected.*

- Operating at a maximum level means thinking big-picture, not small-frame.

- Operating at an A level in a C-level environment can be inhibited by three key things: *time, knowledge,* and *staff.*

- A mentor's goal is to nurture dynamic and fresh talent for greatness. A mentor should be responsible for a mentee's emotional, intellectual, social, spiritual, and fiscal prosperity.

- A strategy is more important than even a compass. A compass is a tool, but a strategy is a plan for using that tool.

- Oftentimes, we unconsciously accept God's call before we consciously accept his direction.

- God always has a direction even if we don't have His marching orders.

- Our duty is to represent God in a way that entices people to desire God in a more intimate way.

- The amount of preparation time is in direct relation to your elevation altitude.

- God's perfect timing is the moment when opportunity and destiny collide.

- In our time of preparation we need to practice the traits needed for our destiny.

- Greatness isn't a spectator sport; it requires active participation.

- Raising my own bar breeds consistency and responsibility in those around me.

- Sweet spot: where passion meets purpose. The biggest indicator of someone *not* operating in their sweet spot is confusion and disorder.

- Excellence attracts excellence. If most of the people I know are average, then I probably am, too; if they are moving toward greatness, then so am I.

- I should ensure friends are pursuing the same level of excellence and greatness as I am.

- Great mentors open doors, create opportunities, and secure resources on behalf of their mentee.

- When setting goals, be adventurous and willing to take risks, but not outrageous.

- All well-thought-out objectives have a timeframe attached. Timeframes help us identify where we are and where we should be by when.

- Rebounding is bouncing or springing back from a force of impact. Every goal and objective should have a recovery strategy.

- God's goal is to get high-capacity activity out of low-capacity people —to move us from our human hierarchy to our heavenly highchair.

Up Next ⇨

Keys to Greatness: Confidence in Self defines confidence, instructs us on fear and how to overcome it, and offers self-assessments on moral values, passions, strengths, weaknesses, peace stealers, and, finally, reframing "negative" traits into positive confidence builders.

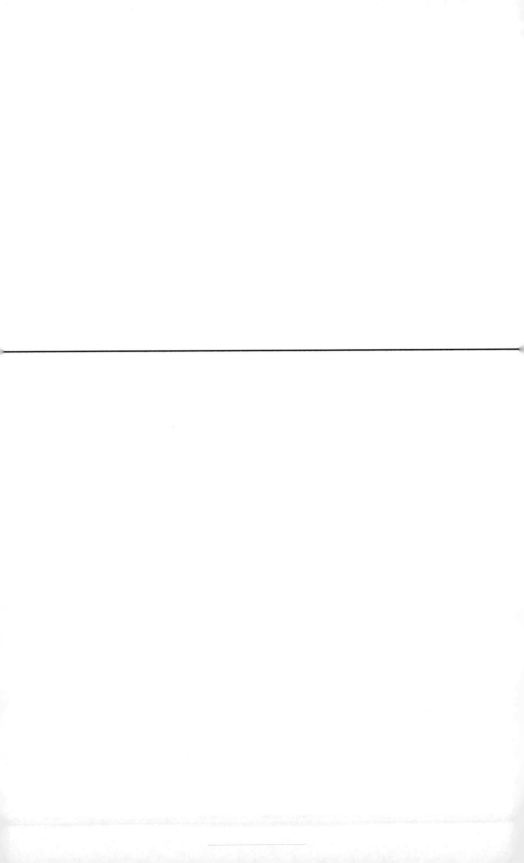

Keys to Greatness: Confidence in Self

Keys to Greatness: Confidence in Self

Self-confidence is believing in one's own abilities even when others don't. Trusting ourselves and being self-assured and confident are essentials for greatness. We are born with 100% confidence, but life's disappointments, heartaches, stresses, and fears erode our self-esteem over the years. Absentee parents, never hearing an encouraging word, low expectations, hostile homes, etc., rob us of our confidence at a young age and often paralyze us in adulthood. My goal in this chapter is to disarm anything that might rob our confidence.

I've had the distinct pleasure of working with many terrific and confident colleagues, and I have noticed that confident people often:

- Address the work at hand;
- Convey and communicate their expectations very clearly;

- Are highly capable and resourceful;

- Contribute something meaningful and relevant;

- Look to your expertise with an open mind, not just to validate what they want to do;

- Don't need to showcase their possessions;

- Weigh options and make solid decisions;

- Assist others with their purpose and goals, even if they themselves might not benefit directly;

- Celebrate the successes of others publicly and privately;

- Use discreet language and nonverbal communication to suggest disapproval (ex: a look, a pause to suggest the conversation has concluded) and are never rude or disrespectful.

Just as the above character traits reflect our confidence, likewise the threats below can decrease our confidence. These little foxes disarm and rob us of confidence and of our greatness.

Fear

Fear is the adversary of greatness. Fear is one of the major reasons people don't live in greatness. Isn't it funny how we are fearless with sin, but cautious with destiny? While some take fearless steps *toward* passion and destiny, others take fearful safe steps *from* passion and destiny. In 1 Samuel 17 (NLT used here), David (one of my all-time favorite Bible characters) demonstrates his fearlessness and sense of adventure and offers keys for our own pursuit of greatness:

- ASK QUESTIONS FIRST. Being fearless means asking thorough questions. "David asked the soldiers standing nearby, 'What will a man get for killing this Philistine and ending his defiance of Israel? Who is this pagan Philistine anyway that he is allowed to defy the armies of the living God?' ...He walked over to some others and asked them the same thing and received the same answer" (verses 26, 30). When afraid, we should ask questions to know exactly what we're up against and to plan the best strategy.

- GOD'S GLORY. The best fear-reducing strategy is to speak the Word. The very Word that Christ preached to thousands is the same Word that will dissuade our fears today. When we seek to elevate the Lord and not ourselves, He gives us courage to face our fears. David wanted to put an end to Goliath's defiance of the Lord, not to promote himself. "You come to me with sword, spear, and javelin, but I come to you in the name of the Lord of Heaven's Armies—the God of the armies of Israel, *whom you have defied*. Today the Lord will conquer you, and I will kill you and cut off your head. And then I will give the dead bodies of your men to the birds and wild animals, and the whole world will know that there is a *God in Israel! And everyone assembled here will know that the Lord rescues His people*, but not with sword and spear. *This is the Lord's battle, and He will give you to us!*" (verses 45-47; emphasis mine). David's confidence increased with each word, like moving up a musical scale. He boldly confronted Goliath even when it looked like all odds were against him. In building our confidence, it helps if we remember and learn from David's motive: for God—not himself—to get the glory.

- WHAT YOU HAVE IS ENOUGH. David was asked to wear the soldier's armor. "'I can't go in these,' he protested to Saul. 'I'm not used to them.' So David took them off again. He picked up five smooth stones from a stream and put them into his shepherd's bag. Then, armed only with his shepherd's staff and sling, he started across the valley to fight the Philistine" (verses 39-40). Seldom does God do a one-size-fits-all. **God gifted you with your own style, gifts, knowledge, experience, personality, and performance.** He wants you to rely on what He's given you to work with and to trust Him completely for the rest.

- DON'T SELF-PROMOTE. "'Well, find out who he is!' the king told [Abner]. As soon as David returned from killing Goliath, Abner brought him to Saul with the Philistine's head still in his hand" (verses 56-57). When David had accomplished the task, the king came looking for him. By the same token, when we do mighty things in the name of God, people will want to know who we are and the secret to our success. **Your actions—not self-promotion—bring accolades.**

Don't let circumstances evoke fear. Fear is an excuse to maintain the status quo. I never want to be in a place where I cannot claim something God has for me because of fear. **We say, "We've always done it this way," but what we're really saying is, "I'm afraid to do it differently."**

The Bible story of Peter stepping out of the boat is one I most treasure. "Lord, if it's you, Peter replied, tell me to come to you on the water. Come, he said. Then Peter got down out of the boat, walked on the water and came toward Jesus. But when he noticed the strong wind, he was frightened. As he began to sink, he shouted, Lord, save me!" (Matthew 14:28-30, NIV). **What's interesting about this story is that it's the things we know that shake us, not the things we don't know.** Peter was a fisherman, so he was familiar with the sea and the wind. It was the *wind* that tested Peter. The *wind*, which I'd like to refer to as circumstances, *comes* to test our faith. **Circumstances bring difficulty and distractions, not the task itself.** Although Peter was later swayed by the wind (his circumstances), it was his faith that had taken him to the next level in the first place.

Greatness requires getting out of the comfort zone and into the unfamiliar. Seeking people's approval and validation involves constantly trying to fit in, going along to get along, but seeking God's approval means making a new fitting to become who you were supposed to be when God created you.

Play to Your Best Attributes

Another key to greatness is to know your best attributes. One such attribute is gender. Way too often, men and women don't play to their gender strengths. This problem is often exacerbated by the morphing of a genderless society. Our gender is God-created, just like our personality. Embrace your masculinity or femininity and all the wonderful qualities being a man or a woman provides. There is a reason children need both parents. The balance between father and mother, man and woman, begins in our home environment but doesn't stop there; it lives on and affects all other aspects of our life.

As a woman, be sensitive. Look to men for protection and provision. Nothing screams masculinity like a man with the ability to provide a safe presence. Man's strength is a trait women still find attractive. Likewise, a woman's gentleness and ability to create a warm and welcoming atmosphere can win over many. As women, we should embrace, not try to hide our femininity. I love the poem "Phenomenal Woman" by Maya Angelou, which models this concept so well. An excerpt reads:

> *Men themselves have wondered*
> *What they see in me.*
> *They try so much*
> *But they can't touch*
> *My inner mystery.*
> *When I try to show them*
> *They say they still can't see.*
> *I say,*
> *It's in the arch of my back,*
> *The sun of my smile,*
> *The ride of my breasts,*
> *The grace of my style.*
> *I'm a woman*
> *Phenomenally.*
> *Phenomenal woman,*
> *That's me.*

I said in Chapter 5 that one of the most challenging, yet important, responsibilities in life is to know yourself. So often, we pretend to know ourselves, but do we really? To know myself is to know both my good and bad qualities, the bright and the dark side of me, the public and the private persona of who I am. If I know who I am and what I want, I have a better chance of figuring out how to achieve my own success, happiness, and personal fulfillment—that is, greatness! How well do you know your best attributes? Answer these questions:

My three best qualities are:

1. _____

2. _____

3. _____

My three worst qualities are:

1. _____

2. _____

3. _____

Three ways I'm different in public than in private/what others might be surprised to learn about me:

1. _____

2. _____

3. _____

In the space below, write a personal advertisement about yourself.

_____

_____

_____

_____

We should be familiar with our moral values, passions, strengths, weaknesses, and things that steal our peace. As we look at each of these individually, fill in the blanks to complete a self-assessment. In fact, if you really want a true assessment, give this exercise to three to five close friends and ask their opinions of you.

Moral Values. Morals are your personal principles or rules of ethical conduct. Everyone has good and bad decisions and actions. We all use different measuring rods for these actions. What or who keeps you from pushing the envelope too far?

- How do you evaluate right and wrong?

- Is there something/someone you use as a guide for life decisions? Who?

- Survey your life: What would you never do even if no one ever found out about it?

Passions. Passions bring strong desire and enthusiasm; a passion might be described as what you would do even if you never made money from it. Passion drives us and excites us.

- My heart pounds with excitement when…

- I feel good about myself when…

- I get a lump in my throat when…

- I lose track of time whenever I am…

- If money were not an issue, I would…

Strengths. A strength is an internal power where you have the most energy. Circle your obvious strengths and place a "B" next to the strengths you would like to build on.

Forthright	Inventive	Thorough
Adventurous	Spontaneous	Dependable
Forceful	Trusting	Self-composed
Sharp	Outgoing	Possessive
Decisive	Unselfish	Analytical
Risk taker	Self-assured	Controlling
Demanding	Charming	Perfectionist
Authoritative	Inspiring	Systematic
Direct	Steady	Conventional
Curious	Amiable	Respectful
Competitive	Predictable	Meticulous
Self-sufficient	Supportive	Well-disciplined
Enthusiastic	Loyal	Diplomatic
Expressive	Methodical	Precise
Influential	Team player	Sensitive
Emotional	Calm	Accurate

Weaknesses. A weakness is an internal realm in which you have the least power or energy. Not only is identifying our strengths important, we must also recognize weak spots that hinder our greatness:

- My friends say I should be better about…

- My supervisor and clients think I should work on my…

- I wouldn't be surprised if people said I was…

- I'm misunderstood about…

Peace Stealers. These are the people and situations that cause us to lose our peace. The key is to recognize potential peace stealers beforehand. Below, please list the people and situations that have stolen your peace in the past. How will you overcome them in the future?

Person/situation that stole my peace	How I will overcome in the future
My rude coworker.	*Pray for her, avoid her when I can.*
Driving in rush hour traffic.	*Listen to soothing music, take an alternate route.*

Build Confidence from Past Accomplishments

Last, a great tool for building self-confidence is examining your past accomplishments and reframing your negative traits. Look over the chart and benchmarks from Chapter 3 or take some time to think back over your life. What are your three greatest accomplishments? (Exclude family and friends.)

1. _____

2. _____

3. _____

Now, reframe your weaknesses to build what I call "confidence conveyors." Confidence conveyors leverage our strengths against our weaknesses.

EXAMPLE: *I am good with people individually but I am not comfortable networking in a group. I can leverage my people skills by initiating a one-on-one conversation when I'm engaged in a group.*

Below, please write a confidence conveyor for each of the following areas of your life:

Spiritual

_____

_____

_____

_____

Personal

_____

_____

_____

_____

Career

_____

_____

_____

_____

Physical

_____

_____

_____

_____

I pray this chapter has been beneficial for defining confidence, identifying confidence builders and stealers, and recognizing and building on past achievements to develop confidence. A confident person truly does display greatness.

Chapter Highlights

- A Self-confident person believes in his or her own abilities even when others don't.

- Trusting ourselves and being self-assured and confident are essentials for greatness.

- Fear is the adversary of greatness.

- God gifted you with your own style, gifts, knowledge, experience, personality, and performance; embrace them.

- Your actions—not self-promotion—bring accolades.

- We say, "We've always done it this way," but what we're really saying is, "I'm afraid to do it differently."

- It's circumstances that bring difficulty, not the task itself.

- Greatness requires getting out of the comfort zone and into the unfamiliar.

- Seeking people's approval and validation involves constantly trying to fit in, going along to get along. Seeking God's approval means making a new fitting to become who you were supposed to be when God created you.

- Our gender is God-created, just like our personality. Embrace your masculinity or femininity and all the wonderful qualities being a man or woman provides.

- Morals are your personal principles or rules of ethical conduct.

- Passions bring strong desire and enthusiasm; they are what you would do even if you never made money from it.

- A strength is an internal power where you have the most energy.

- A weakness is an internal power or force where you have the least energy.

- Peace stealers are the people and situations that cause us to lose our peace.

Up Next ⇨

Keys to Greatness: Confidence in Christ examines more of what is essential for greatness including: accepting our privilege and expecting the best, and understanding that success involves humility, position, and then the promotion.

Keys to Greatness: Confidence in Christ

Keys to Greatness: Confidence in Christ

If it weren't for my trust in God, I wouldn't have the confidence to move forward in my destiny. For years I wanted to write a book and move abroad but never had the courage to do so. Fast-forward to today; as I write this book, I'm in London unpacking and feeling homesick. Like Ruth, it took courage to move from familiarity to confidence and to trust God *completely*. **Yet as my relationship with Christ grows, so does my confidence to step out in faith into unfamiliar territory.** My decision and confidence in God have changed my life and confirmed my calling.

I wasn't always so confident. In fact, shortly after I arrived in London, I started venting to God about being halfway around the world and missing my friends, family, and home. Once, while I was venting, I happened to pull out an old handmade photo frame with the word T.R.U.T.H. written on it. As I looked at the photo frame, I saw that the letter T. had fallen off somehow during my travels, so the frame now said R.U.T.H. Immediately, the biblical Ruth's words to her mother-in-law Naomi came to my mind: "Wherever you go, I will go; wherever you live, I will live. Your people will be my people, and your God will be my God" (Ruth 1:16, NLT). During my stay in London, this verse proved true. Like Ruth, I found myself in a new territory meeting new people. I met Christians from all over the world and traveled to places I had only read about.

While in London I developed my definition of confidence, which is simply *trust in God*—trust in God in the unknown, and trust that God guides us to our destiny. The Bible says in Hebrews 10:35-36 (NIV), "So do not throw away your confidence; it will be richly rewarded. You need to persevere so that when you have done the will of God, you will receive what He has promised." The more we trust in God, the more confident we become in ourselves and our actions. When you have confidence in Christ, you say "yes" to new experiences, new privileges, and new expectations.

Privilege and Expectation

If I had found out yesterday that I was related to the royal family, I would behave differently today. I would speak differently, think differently, and act differently. **Privilege, God's favor, brings a certain sense of expectation.**

Like Jesus, we are born great. Jesus spoke, thought, and acted from His place of privilege, His greatness, and we must do the same. **We must become great for ourselves before others can recognize our greatness.** Ask yourself, what are the privileges and expectations that come with greatness? Does greatness gossip? Is greatness late? Is greatness unfit? Does greatness procrastinate? What does greatness do?

By the same token, Romans 8:32 (NIV) says, "He who did not spare his own Son, but gave him up for us all—how will he not also, along with him, graciously give us all things?" **As children of the King, we should walk with expectation and privilege.** When I am in the right place spiritually and my heart is toward God, I expect people to tell me yes. This is my spiritual confidence. According to scriptures below, our success in life is in direct relation to our belief in God to deliver.

Review the scriptures below (emphasis is my own) and think about what they have in common:

- Mark 9:23 (NKJV) "Jesus said to him, '*If you can believe*, all things are possible to him who believes.'"

- Matthew 17:20 (NKJV) "So Jesus said to them, 'Because of your unbelief; for assuredly, I say to you, *if you have faith* as a mustard seed, you will say to this mountain, Move from here to there, and it will move; and nothing will be impossible for you.'"

- Mark 11:24 (NLT) "I tell you, you can pray for anything, and *if you believe that you've received it, it will be yours.*"

- Matthew 9:28-30 (NLT) "They went right into the house where he was staying, and Jesus asked them, "Do you believe I can make you see?' 'Yes, Lord,' they told him, 'we do.' Then he touched their eyes and said, '*Because of your faith, it will happen.*' Then their eyes were opened, and they could see! Jesus sternly warned them, 'Don't tell anyone about this.'"

- Matthew 8:13 (NLT) "Then Jesus said to the Roman officer, Go back home. '*Because you believed, it has happened.*' And the young servant was healed that same hour."

Belief seems to be dependent on faith with action. This means we cannot have true belief, or prove our belief, unless we do something. The first thing we must do is have faith in God. Why is it easier to believe what everyone else says instead of God? Perhaps because we can't touch God or see Him in physical form. However, *powerful* faith is knowing and trusting what you can't see with the natural eye.

First Corinthians 2:13-16 (NLT) says, "When we tell you these things, we do not use words that come from human wisdom. Instead, we speak words given to us by the Spirit, using the Spirit's words to explain spiritual truths. But people who aren't spiritual can't receive these truths from God's Spirit. It all sounds foolish to them and they can't understand it, for only those who are spiritual can understand what the Spirit means. Those who are spiritual can evaluate all things, but they themselves cannot be evaluated by others. For, 'Who can know the Lord's thoughts? Who knows enough to teach him? But we understand these things, for we have the mind of Christ.'

What Paul is saying here is that spiritual things are discerned by the Spirit. When it comes to faith in God's word, we fall into one of five tiers:

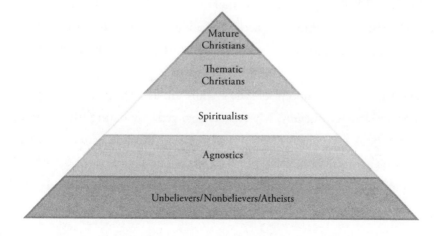

- **Mature Christians** believe the Bible in its entirety, even the parts they don't like. They are committed and submitted to God's word.

- **Thematic Christians** take only the parts of the Bible that they like. They follow God halfway when it's convenient for them. I also like to call these *Smorgasbord* Christians.

- **Spiritualists** believe that there are multiple ways to get to God; any avenue will do. They think it's better to be true to your authentic self.

- **Agnostics** have no proof of the existence of any God. Their motto is, "Just be a good person."

- **Unbelievers/Nonbelievers/Atheists** have no spiritual knowledge or belief in God.

Most people fit in one of the above five faith tiers. Your spiritual expectation is based on where you see yourself spiritually. **No one starts their Christian walk as a fully mature Christian.** I certainly didn't. As in all relationships, spending time and giving effort and dedication enable growth. If we don't work at our relationship with God, it's difficult to move from believing to knowing. **Relationship—not religion—brings privilege and expectation!** Religion is nothing more than checking the box and saying I'm a Christian. It's similar to checking the box of Democrat or Republican, but not knowing the platform, policies, or voting record of the candidate.

When I grasped the concept of who I really am as a child of God, my life started to change…literally. My friends changed, my dating life changed, my checkbook even changed. Everything changed for the better. I stopped worrying and started expecting. We have to put our confidence in Christ and be mindful that challenges will come to test us before we are promoted—our next phase of elevation.

When I was twelve years old I walked into a church, with no prompting from anyone, and gave my life to Christ. There was something calling me, which I now know as the Holy Spirit. After that life-changing moment, I continued to go to church faithfully and without my mother. My mother would drop me off and pick me up systematically because she was not a Christian and had absolutely no interest in joining. My teen and early adult years were full of everything and anything *un*Christian. Eventually in my late twenties, I did find my way back well after I had racked up my share of sinful deeds. The entertainment industry was lacking in role models of purity, character, and integrity; it is, after all, the entertainment industry. I never justified my behavior. I knew I had strayed so far from where God (and I) wanted my life to be, so I continued to do what I wanted to and with whomever. Looking back, I thank God for His mercy and grace…I found my way back to Him.

It's a huge misconception that Christianity equals perfection when, in reality, it's the opposite. It means pursuit of all things God-like: humility, kindness, patience, diligence, charity, self-control, and chastity. **God doesn't need perfect people because perfect people don't need God.** There are no Twelve Steps to Perfect Christianity; that's religion. Just as we as individuals are different, so are our spiritual journeys all different. My path started with the prayer below, and your journey to greatness can start, too, with this beautiful prayer, or yours might begin with something similar to this.

"Father, I know that I have broken your laws and my sins have separated me from you. I am truly sorry, and now I want to turn away from my past sinful life toward you. Please forgive me, and help me avoid sinning again. I believe that your Son, Jesus Christ, died for my sins, was resurrected from the dead, is alive, and hears my prayer. I invite Jesus to become the Lord of my

life, to rule and reign in my heart from this day forward. Please send your Holy Spirit to help me obey you, and to do your will for the rest of my life. In Jesus' name I pray. Amen."

If you prayed this prayer, send me an email and I will send you a special gift to welcome you to the family. If you didn't, you can still send me an email to say hello or ask a question. Towan@chasinggreatness.com ☺.

The Process of Promotion

Success is many things to many people, but I define **success as *our personal measure for a desired outcome.*** One person's idea of success is not the same for all. For some, success is money and things, whereas for others, it could be a healthy marriage and family. Throughout life, I've observed a **consistent development process that occurs en route to success: being humbled, being positioned, and being promoted.**

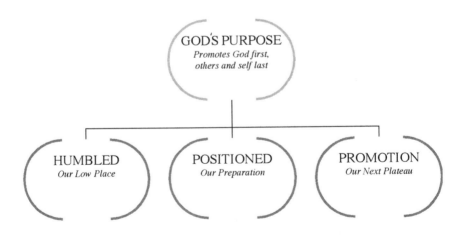

- Humbled: 1 Peter 5:6 (NRSV) says, "Humble yourselves there-fore under the mighty hand of God, so that he may exalt you in due time." The Hebrew word for "humble" means *to submit or become low.* Humbleness is our brokenness or low place where we end and we allow God to begin. It's when we've exhausted our own strength and abilities, and we are finally willing to recognize that only God has our answer.

- Position: Second Chronicles 20:17 (NKJV) says, "You will not need to fight in this battle. Position yourselves, stand still and see the salvation of the Lord, who is with you." Position is *our preparation place.* It's our time of testing, sharpening, pruning...our grooming period before we are catapulted to promotion.

- Promotion: Psalm 75:6-7 (KJV) says, "For promotion cometh neither from the east, nor from the west, nor from the south. But God is the judge: he putteth down one, and setteth up another." Promotion is *where the spirit of faith and God's place of preparation collide.* We begin walking into our season, the fruit of our existence...our destiny—our success.

We often arrive at various stages of this development process simulta-neously in different areas of our lives. When I started my company, I was going through several phases and emotions at the same time. I was humbled financially, positioned emotionally, but promoted spiritually. Each phase strengthened me in different areas. It was in my humble place where I had no choice but to trust God. Humility brings you to your lowest place where there's no escape. I had no other option for money; my accounts were exhausted, I had no clients, and bills were due, including two mortgages. Emotionally I felt like a failure with no other options. Yet, despite being humbled financially, I grew more that year spiritually than ever before. I relied on God for my very existence. I clung to the

Word and prayed constantly. I wasn't the only one to experience this process; there were others throughout the Bible who had the same experience as well:

- In the book of Ruth, we see that Ruth was humbled when her husband died. She had no money and nowhere to go. During Ruth's time of humility she was positioned. She submitted to Naomi's wisdom, increased her faith and trust, and found favor with Boaz. Ruth's promotion arrived when Boaz redeemed her and became her devoted husband. God's purpose for Ruth was nothing short of her son being the grandfather of King David; she became part of the lineage of Christ himself! **Humility, position, and promotion moments are always divinely designed for Christ's purpose, not ours.**

- David was humbled in 1 Samuel 18-31 when he fled from King Saul. David's refuge in Gath and the good relationships he forged with the tribes in the south earned him a position of respect from the southerners. But ultimately, we know that David's greatest promotion was in 2 Samuel 5 when he was crowned king. David's time of preparation enabled him to form alliances and become the supreme diplomat necessary to be a king. David's purpose was to unite the twelve tribes, and his experience in Gath helped prepare him.

Most of the great people I know go through a process of gaining greatness—a process riddled with failures and setbacks that are necessary for success. Many of us don't understand that *a setback really is a setup for a step up.* If we grasp that concept, we move toward God's will and our greatness. **Being humbled, positioned, and promoted is not to defeat us, but to define us.**

Survey your life. Describe how you are being humbled, positioned, and promoted. Think of your spiritual, personal, professional, and financial situations. What do you think God's purpose is in the process?

Area	PROCESS			God's Purpose
	Humbled (low place)	Positioned (preparation)	Promoted (success)	
Ex. Finances	*Income too low, savings depleted.*			*1) God's making me more fiscally responsible.* *2) God's my sole source, not a job*

It's a Heart Issue

The cornerstone of Confidence in Christ is the heart. Proverbs 4:23 (NASB) says, "Watch over your heart with all diligence, for from it flow the springs of life." **The heart is the core of our person, our inner self, our will and understanding and perspective on life.** We are to protect our heart carefully because it is the source of our being. The best way to tell a person's heart is to listen to what they say. Second Corinthians 2:4 (NKJV) says, "For out of much affliction and anguish of heart I wrote unto you with many tears." We act out what's in our heart. Matthew 12:34 (KJV) says, "O generation of vipers [a viper is someone who is malicious or treacherous] how can ye, being evil, speak good things? For out of the abundance of the heart the mouth speaketh." Quite simply, you are what you speak and what you speak is an indicator of your heart.

To Believe or Not to Believe Christ

Choosing Christ will immediately alienate people. Experience has taught me to tell people, "If you want to have a conversation about my belief, I can have one with you if it's an authentic conversation, not an interrogation." This statement immediately puts people in a posture to either listen or criticize. If it's the latter, I won't engage. Instead, I've found success in demonstrating God's greatness to others following what I call the 3D witnessing process (Demonstration, Deeds, and Diction):

- DEMONSTRATION. *Demonstrate* God. Bad attitudes are toxic to our witness. For the most part, I'm a joyful person. I have a great life… not because everything is perfect, but because I choose to be joyful.

Just like I choose what I'm going to wear, I choose to have joy. Joy is contagious…so when people see me happy, they immediately want to know why, and then I hit them with the 1-2 Jesus punch! Be mindful that once you make the decision to demonstrate Christ, temptations to compromise your witness are just around the corner—getting cut off in traffic, an unfair boss, or a disloyal friend.

- DEEDS. In this world where so many people don't feel valued and appreciated, bringing someone a "just because" cup of coffee can be a huge witnessing tool. **People don't always believe what we say, but they know what we do and how we make them feel.** One day I went to lunch at one of those overpriced downtown hot-and-cold-buffet spots. The young lady in front of me, roughly in her 20s, didn't have enough money for her meal and tried to bargain with the cashier. While watching this exchange, I heard the Holy Spirit say, "Pay for her lunch." "No," I thought. I had the money, but I was being selfish. A few seconds later I heard those words again: "Pay for her meal." So I did what I often do: I bargained with God. I thought, *If I call to her and she responds, I'll pay for her meal.* Since she was ten steps ahead, I figured she wouldn't hear me. "Excuse me, miss," I said. She turned. "If you don't have enough, I'll take care of it." I paid for her meal and everyone in the store looked at me as if I were crazy. I said, "God bless you," and quickly excused myself from the café. Although that was not my first time blessing a complete stranger, it reminded me how **the smallest deeds make the greatest impact.**

God provides opportunities for us as Christians to witness and engage others through our deeds. My witnessing deed was buying lunch. My pastor's is buying groceries and leaving them on seniors' or single mothers' doorsteps *anonymously.* **Look for deeds to engage**

others and be a witness for Christ. In this world people want to believe in humanity and civility. We just have to show them it's possible through our deeds.

DICTION. **The very last thing we should do in order to witness is speak.** The difficult part is letting people engage us in a question-and-answer conversation about God because we fear we won't have all of the correct answers. Remember, we are only sowing the seed of the Word, or watering the seed someone else has sown. Our job is not to change them; only God can change people. **We are here to tell others how good God is in our own lives until unbelievers, spectators, and others decide to invite Him into theirs.** Meet people where they are. I answer their questions and if I don't know an answer, I say so and tell them I'll get back to them when I have an answer. Leave them with hope that where they are isn't where they have to stay. Encourage them not only to learn about God, but also to experience God. Tell them to look for Godly moments and encourage them to quiet their life. For so long, I wasn't able to hear God because my life was so loud: loud situations, loud people, overextended emotions, overextended finances, and busyness.

As I matured, I realized that being silent is not the same as being quiet. Being quiet is being still and listening, internally. Before I speak, I listen to what people are saying. Sometimes I repeat what they said to make sure I understand and to let them know I am actively listening. It's like with food: eating and digesting are not the same. Eating is simply putting the food in your mouth and crunching; digesting is ensuring all the vital organs receive the nourishment and nutrients of the food. Listen to what people say, digest it, and then speak.

Confidence in Christ is vital to a dynamic life. **Many of us don't struggle with *what to do*; we struggle with whether we *want to do* anything to change what we do.** Are we strong enough to really believe what God says in His Word? Can our faith sustain a transition to the next promotion level? **Confidence in Christ is a direct reflection of our faith—faith that requires our participation and allows Christ to act in our lives.** Once that faith is active, we become a live advertisement for God. As a live advertisement, we can't help but share what God has done for us (salvation), through us (for others), and with us (our personal spiritual growth).

I conclude with 2 Corinthians 1:10 (NIV): "We have placed our confidence in him, and he will continue to rescue us." Amen.

Chapter Highlights

- As our relationship with Christ grows, so does our confidence to step out in faith into unfamiliar territory.

- The more we trust in God, the more confident we become in ourselves and our actions.

- Privilege, God's favor, brings a certain sense of expectation. As children of the King, we should walk with expectation and privilege.

- We must become great for ourselves before others can recognize our greatness.

- Belief is faith with action. This means we cannot have true belief, or prove our belief, unless we do something.

- No one starts their Christian walk as a fully mature Christian; it's a process.

- Relationship—not religion—brings privilege and expectation! Religion is nothing more than checking the box and saying I'm a Christian.

- We have to put our confidence in Christ and be mindful that challenges will come to test us before we are promoted to our next place.

- God doesn't need perfect people because perfect people don't need God.

- Success is our personal measure for a desired outcome.

- The development process common to success is being humbled, being positioned, and being promoted. Being humbled, positioned, and promoted is not to defeat us but to define us.

- The Hebrew word for "humble" means to submit or become low. Humbleness is our brokenness or low place where we end and we allow God to begin.

- Position is our preparation place. It's our time of testing, sharpening, pruning...our grooming period before we are catapulted to promotion.

- Promotion is where the spirit of faith and God's place of preparation collide. We begin walking into our season, the fruit of our existence... our destiny—our success.

- Humility, position, and promotion moments are always divinely designed for Christ's purpose, not ours.

- A setback really is a setup for a step up.

- The cornerstone of Confidence in Christ is the heart. The best way to tell a person's heart is to listen to what they say.

- We should demonstrate God's greatness by using a 3D approach (Demonstration, Deeds, and Diction).

- People don't always believe what we say, but they know what we do and how we make them feel.

- The smallest deeds can make the greatest impact.

- Look for deeds with which to engage others and be a witness for Christ. In this world people want to believe in humanity and civility. We just have to show them it's possible through our deeds.

- Only God can change people.

- Many of us don't struggle with *what to do*; we struggle with whether we *want to do* anything to change what we do.

- Confidence in Christ is a direct reflection of our faith—faith that requires our participation and allows Christ to act in our lives. Once that faith is active, we become a live advertisement for God.

Up Next ⇒

Claiming and Possessing Greatness reviews our discomfort in present circumstances and our discomfort in understanding that sometimes we have to "go it alone."

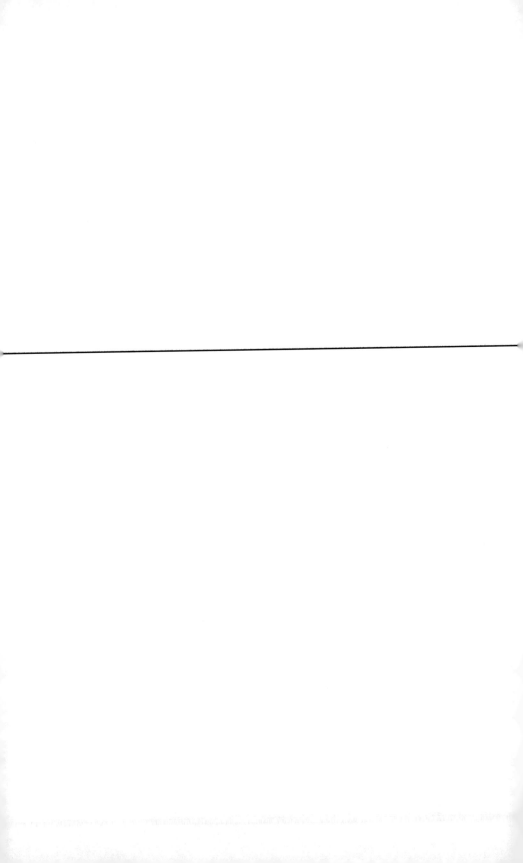

Claiming and Possessing Greatness

CHAPTER 9
Claiming and Possessing Greatness

We must insist that our faith be so strong we don't allow circumstances to compromise our trust in God. As I continue to evolve, my ability to successfully produce is directly enhanced by *knowing* and not anticipating the outcome. I have to be confident that God will provide. It's not an option, but a certainty. It requires a mental shift, an unyielding trust in God. I can promise you that our lives will always be plagued by inconvenient circumstances. These inconvenient circumstances are indicators that alert us that something is wrong and can potentially teach us valuable lessons to take us closer to greatness. The life of Abraham (initially known as Abram), recounted in Genesis 13:1-18 offers insight into claiming and possessing what God has for us. Let's examine how Abraham's life shows us that **people, environments, and decisions can either distance us from or lead us closer to our destiny.**

Genesis 13:1-18 (NRSV):

So Abram went up from Egypt, he and his wife, and all that he had, and Lot with him, into the Negeb. Now Abram was very rich in live- stock, in silver, and in gold. He journeyed on by stages from the Negeb as far as Bethel, to the place where his tent had been at the beginning, between Bethel and Ai, to the place where he had made an altar at the first; and there Abram called on the name of the Lord.

Now Lot, who went with Abram, also had flocks and herds and tents, so that the land could not support both of them living together; for their possessions were so great that they could not live together, and there was strife between the herders of Abram's livestock and the herders of Lot's livestock. At that time the Canaanites and the Perizzites lived in the land. Then Abram said to Lot, "Let there be no strife between you and me, and between your herders and my herders; for we are kindred. Is not the whole land before you? Separate yourself from me. If you take the left hand, then I will go to the right; or if you take the right hand, then I will go to the left."

Lot looked about him, and saw that the plain of the Jordan was well watered everywhere like the garden of the Lord, like the land of Egypt, in the direction of Zoar; this was before the Lord had destroyed Sodom and Gomorrah. So Lot chose for himself all the plain of the Jordan, and Lot journeyed eastward; thus they separated from each other. Abram settled in the land of Canaan, while Lot settled among the cities of the Plain and moved his tent as far as Sodom. Now the people of Sodom were wicked, great sinners against the Lord.

The Lord said to Abram, after Lot had separated from him, "Raise your eyes now, and look from the place where you are, northward and southward and eastward and westward; for all the land that you see I will give to you and to your offspring forever. I will make your offspring like the dust of the earth; so that if one can count the dust of the earth, your offspring also can be counted. Rise up, walk through the length and the breadth of the land, for I will give it to you." So Abram moved his tent, and came and settled by the oaks of Mamre, which are at Hebron; and there he built an altar to the Lord.

Abraham's life teaches us several things:

- Our discomfort is often a signal that brings a new direction;
- Everything that looks good isn't always in our best interest;
- Sometimes we have to "go it alone" and it's in our solitude that God speaks and perfects us;
- We must seize our inheritance by claiming our authority over what rightfully belongs to us;
- We must never be afraid to destroy what keeps us from our very greatness.

Discomfort Often Brings New Direction

The first lesson we learn is that discomfort often brings new direction. Look at Genesis 13:7-9: "and there was strife between the herders of Abram's livestock and the herders of Lot's livestock. At that time the Canaanites and the Perizzites lived in the land. Then Abram said to Lot, 'Let there be no strife between you and me, and between your herders and my herders; for we are kindred. Is not the whole land before you? Separate yourself from me. If you take the left hand, then I will go to the right; or if you take the right hand, then I will go to the left.'"

Friction is often an indication that something needs our attention.

The ability to recognize and decipher life's landmines before stepping on them saves time, resources, and stress, and enables us to move toward greater achievements. How many times have we been able to see things coming around the corner, yet we still chose to move toward the head-on collision?

Abraham and Lot knew trouble was brewing. We can learn from Abraham's actions to value others' opinions even when we don't agree with their methods or beliefs. **Division comes when you don't respect others' opinions.** Although bickering is usually an indicator of a deeper issue, it is possible for people to hold different opinions without being divisive. Being diplomatic isn't the same as aligning yourself with others' views. **You don't have to agree, but you can listen and respect the other person's point of view.** Abraham took the high road to keep the peace. Doing so demonstrates a greater sense of humanity.

Last year I surveyed my life and listed every person (including family members) who moved me *toward* my destiny and those who moved me *from* my destiny. After completing the exercise, I realized that the tension spots in my life were the direct result of people who were moving me *from* my destiny. This small exercise has been highly effective in helping me improve my more challenging relationships.

List below the key people you communicate with on a regular basis. Check the column that applies to those relationships today. Are they taking you *toward* your destiny or *from* your destiny? Over the next few months, put the "from destiny" relationships on "code red." Explore what, if anything, you can do to salvage, improve, or remove these relationships. Make this assessment at the end of each year.

Person's name	Toward destiny	From destiny	Steps to change relationship

The more we choose to be laden with difficult relationships, the more time and energy it takes away from our potential greatness. Instead we should be using that time to focus on relationships that move us toward destiny. Some relationships were never meant to be in the first place. For example, some men should be boyfriends and some should be husbands; some women should be girlfriends and some should be wives. Some individuals aren't intended to be our best friends, yet we can still treat them respectfully as colleagues. Some acquaintances are best kept at acquaintance level because if we allow them to ascend to the level of friend, it will be a one-sided, draining relationship that hinders, rather than enhances, our growth. **If you perceive signs of discomfort in a relationship, view them as indicators that God is opening a door for new direction in your life.**

Not Everything That Looks Good Is Good

Genesis 13:10-11: "Lot looked about him, and saw that the plain of the Jordan was well watered everywhere like the garden of the Lord, like the land of Egypt, in the direction of Zoar; this was before the Lord had destroyed Sodom and Gomorrah. So Lot chose for himself all the plain of the Jordan, and Lot journeyed eastward; thus they separated from each other." Lot selected this valley because it looked good, but in the long run it turned out not to be the best choice. Learn to look beyond the first impression of what looks good and easy.

Too often we make decisions based on appearance or perceived level of difficulty or value. I've learned that the projects that seem at first glance to be the easiest are often the most challenging and stressful. These projects sometimes net the least income. Other times projects I initially thought would be challenging are easier and more fun. Instead of making decisions based on first impressions, we should base decisions on where we are going.

Genesis 13:14: "After Lot left, the Lord said to Abram, "From where you are, look carefully in all directions" (verse 14). **We, too (figuratively), are heading North, South, East, or West.** Use the image below as a life compass that enables us to determine the direction of our lives. North is looking ahead...where I am going, my destiny. South is previous experience...where I came from. East represents people, places, and things that take me *from* God and away from my destiny. West represents people, places, and things that take me *toward* God to my destiny. When we are truly in communion with God and living in God's will, our lives will be moving toward the best place, our destiny.

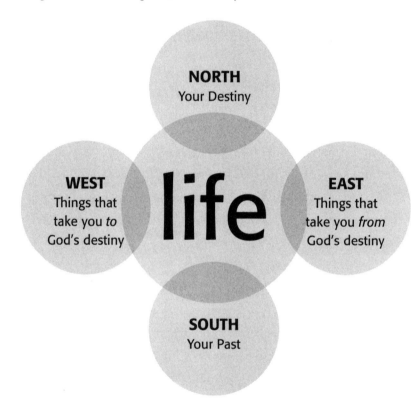

In the old Western movies, the saying *Go West* meant a better opportunity, freedom, and greater resources—prosperity. It's time we embraced a *Go West* mindset. A *Go West* mindset starts with intention. We are the only human constant in our lives; everything else comes and goes and passes away. It's safe to say, **"If my life isn't living up to my expectations, I need to change it."** But our ability to look—and indeed to move—beyond our current situation determines whether we *Go West*, move South by reliving the past, or go East away from God. Then, too, sometimes we stay still and nothing happens.

Your life today is the summation of your decisions yesterday. Live with intention. Change your mind and you'll change your life. Develop a plan to ensure that every aspect of your life is in order to claim an inheritance of greatness.

North	East	South	West
Based on what you know of your gifts, talents, and experience, what would you say is your destiny?	What bad habits compromise your destiny?	Who or what do you need to forgive and/or forget from your past that causes you to doubt your ability to be competent in your destiny?	Starting today, what three things do you need to start doing to take you to your destiny?

Sometimes We Have to Go Alone

In verse 9, Abraham tells Lot, "Is not the whole land before you? Separate yourself from me. If you take the left hand, then I will go to the right; or if you take the right hand, then I will go to the left." **Sometimes God gives us solo directions.** Alone time with God enables Him to work on us personally and gives Him our undivided attention without feedback and input from others. Destiny is a personal journey. Not only can others not always come with you; they may not be able to handle your promise.

Imagine if God said, "Next year you will be wealthier than Oprah." What would people say? Can others handle your promise without it causing them to feel inept about creating their own dynamic life?

The wrong person's input is detrimental to our greatness. Nothing demonstrates this more than children whose hope, life, and destiny are restricted by their parents' criticism. Imagine all the incredible singers who didn't audition for *American Idol* because others discouraged them, or brilliant youth who didn't apply to college because someone said they weren't smart enough. When we listen to people too long, we start to believe them instead of God. **People can't dream beyond their capacity to understand their own potential and promise.** So you know you can't depend on other people to see your promise. Lot honestly couldn't comprehend the Promised Land the way Abraham could, so Abraham had to "go it alone."

Claim Your Inheritance

God said to Abraham, "All the land that you see I will give to you and your offspring forever. I will make your offspring like the dust of the earth, so that if anyone could count the dust, then your offspring could be counted. Go, walk through the length and breadth of the land, for I am giving it to you" (verses 15-16).

If someone gave me the keys to their million-dollar mansion and allowed me to stay for the weekend, I would be thankful. But if someone gave me the keys and the deed, my attitude and behavior would be completely different. **I would have an *owner* mentality instead of an *occupant* mindset.** If there is no change of mind, there can be no change of circumstances. An *owner* mindset enables you to claim the Father's inheritance and supernatural blessings as your God-given inheritance.

A crucial component to claiming your inheritance is to remember that if it's not God's will, you cannot claim it. Apart from God, we are nothing but our empty, shallow selves with no purpose and no power. We walk around laying hands on material things, claiming other people's spouses, buying homes we can't afford, and perpetuating an image with the intent of pleasing others. Like a coat claim check, I can only pick up *my coat* with *my ticket*. Likewise, we can only claim the will of God for our lives.

We cannot understand the will of God unless we have a relationship with God. Greater intimacy with God yields a better understanding of His will. The closer I am with Him, the more I trust and expect He will do what's in my best interest even if I don't know what that interest is myself. The more time I spend with my parents, the deeper understanding I gain of who they are, what they value, and who I am as a reflection of them. Likewise, how can I know God's will if I don't spend time with Him?

Knowing God means removing the word *but* from your vocabulary. I can't say, "I want to, Lord, *but* I have so many bills. I know you said he's not the one, *but* I'm almost 40." Trust God, who said through the prophet Isaiah, "He that putteth his trust in me shall possess the land, and shall inherit my holy mountain" (Isaiah 57:13, KJV).

When I walk with God, there is a difference between speculation and confirmation, between believing and knowing. In order for God to really show His glory, He wants us to expect His will. As we learned earlier, Caleb's attitude was different from that of the other Israelite spies. Caleb insisted they could take and conquer the land, and because of Caleb's attitude of expectation, his descendents possessed God's promise—claimed their inheritance. We must be eager to do the same.

Claiming by Destroying

I often wonder why claiming and destroying are sometimes used synonymously in the Bible. Micah 4:13 (NIV) says, "Rise and thresh, O Daughter of Zion, for I will give you horns of iron; I will give you hoofs of bronze and you will break to pieces many nations. You will devote their ill-gotten gains to the LORD, their wealth to the Lord of all the earth."

I believe God has us destroy the very things that can potentially hold us hostage. In 1 Samuel 15:3 (KVJ) God told Saul, "Now go and smite Amalek, and utterly destroy all that they have, and spare them not; but slay both man and woman, infant and suckling, ox and sheep, camel and ass." But Saul did not listen. Instead he disobeyed and did what he wanted to do. He did not destroy what he perceived to be the best sheep, oxen, and camels. He kept them for himself. **When God asks us to completely remove something, it's because he's able to see the whole movie, while we only see the trailer.**

When God asks us to destroy something, He wants it completely removed to test our commitment to Him. Saul's disobedience caused God to reject him.

I don't want to relinquish God's eternal best because I wouldn't cut out what I thought was good. **Completely remove whatever God says needs to be destroyed in order to claim your greatness.**

Righteousness and Possession

How many of us want *all* the blessings God has for us, yet are not following His principles? To become *righteous is to adhere to Godly principles.* The Greek translation for *righteous* is *dike* (pronounced "dee kay"). It implies *justice* and *conformance to established standards.* Justice means "doing the right thing," and conformance to established standards (in the Bible) refers to "following the ways of God." Deuteronomy 5:33 (KJV) says, "Ye shall walk in all the ways which the LORD your God hath commanded you, that ye may live, and that it may be well with you, and that ye may prolong your days in the land which ye shall possess."

Righteousness involves several truths:

- **If you really want to be righteous, you can be.** Matthew 5:6 (NIV) says, "Blessed are those who hunger and thirst for righteousness, for they will be filled." If I hunger for righteousness, I will become more righteous.

- **Righteousness involves living for God's Kingdom, not ourselves.** Matthew 6:33 (NIV) says, "But seek first his kingdom and his righteousness, and all these things will be given to you as well." **Be more concerned about God's Kingdom and less concerned with man's standard.** Get in tune to what God desires and fully embrace His righteousness to take possession of God's promise.

- **The things you do prove whether you are righteous.** Matthew 11:19 (NIV): "But wisdom is proved right by her actions." For a Christian, time itself doesn't produce maturity; time in relationship and communication with God the Father does.

- **The things that you say prove whether you are righteous.** Romans 3:4 (NIV): "Not at all! Let God be true, and every man a liar. As it is written: 'So that you may be proved right when you speak and prevail when you judge.'" The words we use indicate where we are spiritually and emotionally. Shrewd politicians know their words make or break their political campaigns. Our character screams through our verbal and nonverbal communication.

- **Righteous people are at peace with others.** James 3:18 (KJV): "And the fruit of righteousness is sown in peace of them that make peace." **Righteous people are above foolishness; they operate in peace rather than drama.** They possess a purity of mind. Their spirits promote an attitude of excellence; theirs is a royal and almost regal attitude.

- **You have to be an honest judge to be found righteous.** John 7:24 (KJV): "Judge not according to the appearance, but judge righteous judgment." Learn to look below the surface and ask questions. Don't be influenced by the superficial. Not everything that looks good is good.

- **A righteous person has faith in God and His promises.** Romans 3:28 (NIV): "For we maintain that a person is justified by faith apart from observing the law." **God loves it when we move forward in faith, knowing with certainty He will deliver.** To God our faith is a fragrant perfume called *Trust*.

Complete the questions below. Be honest.

- Do you sincerely want to be righteous or do you feel that's what you "should" be?

- Do you live for God or yourself? With most of your decisions, do you consider God first?

- Are your acts righteous or self-promoting?

- Are your words righteous or critical? Is what you say more encouraging or discouraging?

- Are you at peace with those around you or is there mostly friction?

- Are you honest in words and action all the time or only when it doesn't compromise your agenda?

- Do you have faith in what God has promised you or do you simply say so because it's what you "should" say?

Only certainty allows you to claim and possess the place you *will* occupy. Certainty brings confidence that doubt doesn't. Doubt debilitates our expectation. When we move forward with the expectation of an outcome, we move toward what *will* be, not what *could* be.

Chapter Highlights

- Securing your destiny can be extremely difficult when people, environments, and decisions take you further from your best life.

- Friction is often an indication that something needs our attention. Look for signs of discomfort as an indication of God opening a door for new direction.

- The ability to recognize and decipher life's landmines before stepping on them saves time, resources, and stress, and enables us to move toward greater achievements.

- Division comes when you don't respect others' opinions. You don't have to agree, but you can listen and respect the other person's point of view.

- Learn to look beyond the first impression. Too often we make decisions based on initial appearance or perceived level of difficulty or value.

- We are, figuratively, either heading North, South, East, or West in our lives.

- Your life today is the summation of your decisions yesterday. Live with intention. Change your mind and you'll change your life.

- Sometimes God gives us solo directions. Destiny is a personal journey.

- The wrong person's input is detrimental to our greatness. When we listen to people too long, we can start to believe them instead of God.

- People can't dream beyond their capacity to understand their potential and promise.

- Embrace an *owner* mentality instead of an *occupant* mindset. An owner mentality claims the right to your God-given inheritance.

- A crucial component to claiming your inheritance is to remember that if it's not God's will, you cannot claim it.

- We cannot understand the will of God unless we have a relationship with God. Greater intimacy with God yields a better understanding of His will.

- Knowing God means removing the word *but* from your vocabulary. When I walk with God, there is a difference between speculation and confirmation, between believing and knowing.

- When God asks us to completely remove something, it's because he's able to see the whole movie, while we only see the trailer.

- Being righteous means adhering to Godly principles.

- Be more concerned about God's Kingdom and less concerned with man's standard.

- For a Christian, time itself doesn't produce maturity; time *in relationship* and communication with God the Father does.

- The words we use indicate where we are spiritually and emotionally.

- Righteous people are above foolishness; they operate in peace rather than drama.

- Learn to look below the surface and ask questions. Not everything that looks good is good.

- God loves it when we move forward in faith, knowing with certainty He will deliver.

Up Next ⇨

Leading with Greatness outlines specific qualities of great leaders, how to be servant leaders, how to find the right people for your team, tactics for working with difficult people, and exploring basic decision-making principles and time-management strategies.

Leading with Greatness

CHAPTER 10
Leading with Greatness

Great leaders practice several principles that mediocre leaders don't. Such principles center on service, team building, decision making, access, and influence. These leaders pride themselves on creating an environment that isn't selfishly motivated, but rather one that fosters support and encouragement for others. **Great leaders know how to find the right people to lead and create environments for learning, growth, and self-discovery.** They make strategic decisions that keep the end in mind, not the interim. They seek access to resources instead of money and their goal is to influence others more than to gain power and importance—all while pursuing their own ambitions and building their team's capacity.

Serving

Ramman Kenoun says, "Good leaders serve the interests of their people, while unfit leaders exploit their citizens to serve their own" (www.pithypedia. com). **Most people tend to think leadership is about being on top and guiding others. Actually, leadership is being on the bottom and pushing others to the top.** Hospitals serve patients, CEOs serve shareholders, restaurants serve customers, Jesus served people; **a leader's job is to serve his team.** If we are not serving, we are not leading… successfully. Effective leaders have a servant's heart; they appreciate the needs of others.

The most dynamic leaders are able to keep the objectives and goals of the project in the forefront, yet support and encourage the team by supplying the team's needs and building on the team's capability and capacity. There is a subtle difference between capability and capacity. **Capability is the skill set one has gained from past experiences, while capacity builds on future potential.** Capability should not be the sole deciding factor during the hiring process but it should be considered. In other words, it's a matter of considering not simply where someone is now, but also where they can grow to be later.

That's where the leader comes in. People grow and evolve because of great leaders. **Great leaders not only provide intellect, but also inspiration. A gifted leader isn't always concerned about what they can get; they value what they can give—of their experience, education, and excellence.** This leader seeks to become less prominent by cultivating employees and helping them surpass their previous accomplishments. Their presence makes people stretch up toward higher goals. They know that while they become a staple in the employee's career, they are also serving as an architect and resource for further career building.

Finding the Right People

Recently, I emailed someone on my team a document and asked them to make changes and fax it back. They responded, "I don't have a fax." My rebuttal: "Go to Kinko's!" Did I really need to say that? Yes. Unfortunately, I had made the mistake of hiring someone who, when asked to do something, gave excuses for why they couldn't, rather than coming up with a solution. Experience has taught me to look for those who find solutions, not those who make excuses. The solution response I was looking for was, "I don't have a fax machine, but I'll go to Kinko's."

As an entrepreneur, I can't be everywhere, so delegating becomes necessary to grow a successful organization. Identifying people and delegating responsibility isn't always easy for the leader. The key is identifying people who are self-sufficient and don't require a great deal of micromanagement. Great leaders surround themselves with good people. Often, knowing how much to delegate can be a challenge.

Using the pyramid to the right, you can **identify up-and-coming individuals and their appropriate responsibility levels. Develop a delegation plan for future leaders in your organization (whom to delegate to, what to delegate, and how much to delegate).**

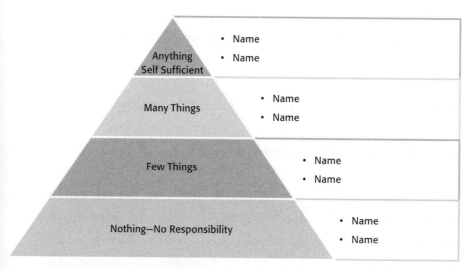

Level of Responsibility

Anything—I like to call this group the superstars. These individuals should be groomed for the next level. They require little to no supervision other than regular assessment meetings. This group is capable of running the operation. This is not the time to feel threatened; you should trust the superstars on your team. They enable you to have greater balance in your life, comfortably spend more time with your family, get advanced degrees, and pursue other ambitions. Superstars make your job easier. Consider them assets. If you are influential in their growth, they're extremely loyal. They are capable of moving directly into your position because you pushed them to their potential. Be discreet in your admiration for these superstars; you don't want to create friction among other team members. Teach them the politics and how to play the game, and all will be well with the world.

Many Things—This group can be trusted with critical tasks. With clear direction and regular supervision, they are poised for leadership. More observation and hands-on experience will propel them to the category of *Anything*.

Although not as seasoned, this group is up-and-coming. Time and experiences will prepare them for their next level.

Few Things—This group can be trusted with just that: managing a *few things* that aren't critical to the organization's overall structure, goal, or growth. They require supervision with weekly updates.

Nothing—This group is at the bottom of the delegation pyramid; they have little to no ability to take responsibilty for a task and cannot function without explicit direction and close, daily supervision. You have to guide them every step of the way. This group tests your leadership ability and patience... lots of prayer, lots of prayer.

Survey your team and identify whom you can assign the least responsibility and on up to the greatest responsibility. **A dynamic leader can grow a team member from no responsibility to full responsibility** ...they build superstars. Be mindful that position doesn't determine success. I've witnessed secretaries run circles around Harvard and Wharton MBAs, and interns run circles around managers.

As a leader, you become indirectly responsible for the emotional development of your team. Nothing destroys a team like envy or jealousy among its members. **A strong team is one where all members are secure with themselves, their abilities, and the talent they each bring.** Secure people often exhibit the following qualities:

- Possess a presence that captivates attention;

- Don't over-speak, are to the point, and keep conversation relevant to the subject matter at hand;

- Don't need to showcase their possessions, nor do they need abundant accolades;

- Assist others with their purpose and don't feel slighted by the accomplishments of others;

- Give their undivided attention and eye contact when communicating;

- Are able to connect and be compassionate without being phony;

- Have an even-tempered voice and use verbal and nonverbal communication to suggest disapproval…a look, a pause, a stare, a smile, to suggest disapproval or approval.

Continue to look for opportunities to strengthen these areas by highlighting team members' individual accomplishments, whether large or small. More important, personally model the self-confidence and secure leadership you want them to embody.

Working with Difficult People

One of the most important leadership skills to develop is working well with people, all people—difficult, crazy, envious, and insecure. I work with many challenging personality types. In working with people, I realize that their insecurities can be their greatest antagonists. Struggles in their personal lives often manifest at work. **Leaders must learn to exercise patience and look below the surface to see the root of the real issue.** Use the strategies below to engage and win people:

- Be clear and direct, and state your expectations clearly.

- Help people feel valued.

- Be willing to help them more than they help you.

- Have targeted comments relevant to subject matter.

- Celebrate accomplishments and successes.

- Give your undivided attention and keep eye contact when communicating.

- Keep an even-tempered voice and use all forms of communication, verbal and nonverbal.

- Have a destiny and direction for the team, project, or cause.

- Make decisions based on God's Word and the facts, and not emotion.

Are You Meeting Your Team's Needs?

Creflo Dollar says, **"In any relationship the four basic human needs are *acceptance, identity, security,* and *purpose"*** (www.creflodol larministries.org). This includes the relationships between leaders and team members.

- **Acceptance** (knowing you are loved and needed by others). We show acceptance by embracing people with no *buts*—loving people even if they never change, taking them as they are with all their shortcomings and past indiscretions.

- **Identity** (knowing you are individually significant and special). Other than knowing God, knowing and loving oneself is most essential for greatness. When we create an identity in response to someone else's idea of who we should be, we are not being authentic to ourselves. A personal cause-and-effect such as *Because they did* this, *I will never* *do* that; *I will become the opposite* undermines your potential greatness. Your identity is just that…yours. Don't let it be manipulated or altered by someone else.

- **Security** (knowing you are well-protected and provided for). Security takes many forms—not just physical protection, but emotional as well. Can this person be trusted with my deepest vulnerabilities and insecurities, or will they use them against me? Will this person be there at any cost? Relationships that allow you to be completely exposed are possible, but few people have yet to experience these authentic relationships, even married couples. Security is freedom from danger or risk. The best hope for security is by taking a self-assessment and building our own set of values that define what's important and then building relationships with people who share those values.

- **Purpose** (knowing you have a reason to live). **Man's greatest reward is knowing why he was put on this earth.** This is not just about your occupation, but who you were born to be and what you were born to leave and contribute for those who come after you. Purpose ties closely with what **my pastor has said are the only three major decisions we will ever make: our maker, our mission, and our mate.** We decide to acknowledge our maker when we accept Jesus Christ as our Lord and Savior. We must decide on our mission because it determines the course of our life. Finally, we will make a decision about our mate—the one with whom we will spend the rest of our life (or, perhaps, *whether* we will choose a mate at all).

Bearing in mind these four basic human needs, how can you as a leader ensure your team is well cared for in these regards? Ask yourself the following questions regularly:

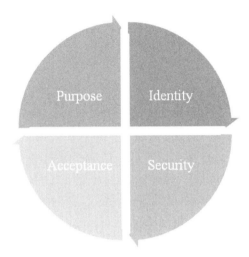

IS IT MUTUALLY BENEFICIAL? Ensure goals are mutually beneficial to all involved. How often do we think, *So, what's in it for me*? For example, if we add two more clients, sure, it's more work, but employees get a day off, the company earns more, and employees receive bonuses. **Showing team members that what's good for the whole is also beneficial for the individual is a key leadership skill.** This doesn't only apply to professional relationships but holds true for personal relationships as well.

WHAT'S YOUR OFFENSIVE STRATEGY? Are you one of those individuals who goes toe to toe with difficult people? **When dealing with difficult people, I've found it better to be offensive rather than defensive.** Offensive strategies require thinking through the situation before reacting, anticipating the other's objections, and remembering to try to touch their heart and not to hurt. Leaders must be able to assess what brings value to the other person. If I take the time to dig deep, I can find their treasure, what motivates them. Listen for their first response and build from there to assess where they place the most value.

HOW TO DEAL WITH CONFLICT? When attempting to deal with difficult people, sometimes conflicts occur. **Disagreements don't have to be destructive or divisive.** I've worked with numerous executives and witnessed many leadership styles. The leaders most celebrated are the ones who can recruit good talent, empower such individuals to make strategic decisions, and reprimand employees in such a way that employees see the error of their ways and are motivated to improve.

It's important to note that reprimanded employees who recover without jeopardizing their relationship with their supervisor prove to be excellent leaders themselves. For them it's not personal; it's about growing. **Imagine the companies we'd have if reprimands were seen as opportunities for growth instead of browbeating and criticism.** Employing the following strategies will make the conflict more constructive:

- **Know the spirit of the person before you engage them.** Notice I said "spirit" and not "personality." The spirit reveals *why*; the personality reveals *who*. *Why* is born from misappropriated intentions—an anticipated outcome that never manifested. *Who* is the character of the person. It's possible to have conflict between well-intentioned individuals.

- Determine the person's intention: Was it to engage a response, provoke thought, protect an action, support efforts, promote their personal agenda, or shoot down another person's idea?

- Set a desired outcome before engaging in conversation. Emotionally infused conversations can go anywhere; let the conversation take the direction you want it to. Keep everything focused and logical to achieve a productive outcome. **Consider what's fair (free from bias) and what's reasonable (what's likely to happen).**

- Think before you speak. Keep what you think in your mind and what you say out of your mouth separate. I have a set of what I like to call *crazy people responses* to keep me from jumping on the table and saying what's really on my mind. Often while in a meeting I'll think, "You must be crazy." What comes out of my mouth is, "Hmmm, really, how do you propose that?" or "Let me think about that" or "That's interesting."

- **Employ some LUV (*Listen, Understand,* and *Validate*) in your communication:** *Listen* to what people say. Listening is concentrating and giving undivided attention, not waiting to talk. *Understand* by repeating what they said to be sure you've heard correctly and are able to argue their point even if it's not your own. *Validate* the other person's feelings.

There is a difference between having opposing views and being divisive. I want people to come to work, do their job, and go home, but people are delicate. **It is human nature to want to be appreciated and valued, so make them feel appreciated and valued.** Taking just five minutes to express concern about their school, family, or project can work wonders in a challenging professional or personal relationship. Five minutes of personal interest can get you two hours of extra work and dedication.

Making Decisions

We make decisions every day. But what do we consider when making decisions? I propose that as we go about our day-to-day decision-making process we follow Solomon's example. Solomon had a three-step systematic approach for making decisions, according to 1 Kings 3:9 (KJV): "Give therefore thy servant an understanding heart [wisdom] to judge thy people, that I may discern [discernment] between good and bad [truth]: for who is able to judge this thy so great a people?" It takes three things to make a decision: wisdom, truth, and discernment.

When purchasing my first home, I considered these three things in my decision making. First, I had little *wisdom* or knowledge about home buying. What did home ownership entail and what were its pros and cons? In order to attain *wisdom*, I educated myself by collecting as much information as possible to increase my level of understanding. Second, I had no *truth*, no point of reference because I had never purchased a home before. So I spoke to people who were homeowners and gleaned from their experiences... the benefits and consequences of home ownership. Last and most important, I prayed for discernment. It's possible to have all the education and experience we need, and for God still to say "no" or "not now." I needed God's confirmation...was it my time, was this a good investment, am I being responsible, should I move? Two months later and with no money down, I became a first-time home owner in what is now one of the swankest areas in Washington, D.C., but it didn't happen until I had applied this three-step process in my decision making.

- Wisdom (point of aptitude, our knowledge)
- Truth (point of reference, perspective based on experience)
- Discernment (seeking God's heart in our decision making, or our spiritual confirmation)

As a business owner, hiring consultants is another activity that requires me to look at all three aspects: 1) *Wisdom:* What is their level of knowledge about a particular project?; 2) *Truth*: What is their experience when it comes to this particular project?; and 3) *Discernment*: What does God tell me about their character, and will they be a good complement to the team?

One would think that decision making would be easier than it is, and that I would not have to put pen to paper about the concept of making smart decisions, but since decision making is, in fact, tricky, I am including this section as a sort of *How to Make Decisions 101*. When engaging the three-step decision-making approach above and the problem-solving model below, one must consider the *best outcome*, what outcome benefits all parties involved, and a *terrible outcome*, what doesn't benefit anyone. Most outcomes will benefit one person more than the other(s). In cases where it turns out we don't benefit as greatly as we had hoped, we must look for and focus on the long-term benefits that will supersede our short-term disappointment.

If an opportunity that yields more money comes along but takes me away from my family, then maybe it's not the best deal for me at the time. Working absurd hours and chasing money, only to lose what you earned, along with your family, in a nasty divorce isn't the best in the long run. Go home and find balance. Think long-term and consider the big picture when making your decision, instead of just thinking of the short-term increase in money.

The diagram at the right illustrates a four-dimensional decision-making process based on four concerns: 1) if our decision will please God, 2) how our decision will impact others, 3) how the decision will impact self, and 4) whether the decision will compromise our relationship with Christ and potentially compromise our character.

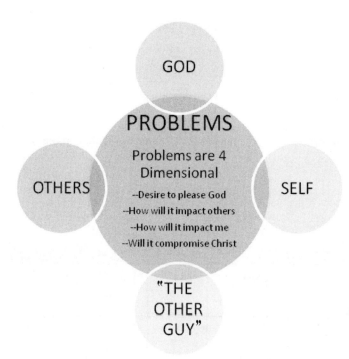

Not every decision will have a successful outcome. Don't look at a disappointment as a defeat, but as an opportunity to refine your position. Our job as leaders is to ensure all outcomes follow the guidelines we have set for ourselves and, if nothing else, uphold our personal values and conditions.

Personal Constitutions

After we make a decision, we must live with it, sometimes for the rest of our lives. Just as the United States has its Constitution to guide its leaders and citizens, as individuals we have personal **constitutions by which we govern ourselves.** Unlike virtues which are universal, **pillars are the core of our own, personal existence.** Pillars are specific to the kind of person we want to be and how we want others to see us. They not only represent what we believe, but also show how we display what we believe. We should all have a personal constitution; it's the pulse of our existence and lets us know when we've moved beyond where we said we would never go. I question people who have no personal constitution because they have no boundaries, no limits. Below, list seven pillars that make up your personal constitution.

THE PILLARS IN MY PERSONAL CONSTITUTION ARE:						
I hereby hold these personal truths to be self-evident, that I will:						
Pillar 1. I will	Pillar 2. I will	Pillar 3. I will	Pillar 4. I will	Pillar 5. I will	Pillar 6. I will	Pillar 7. I will
I will never:	I will never:	I will never:	I will never:	I will never:	I will never:	I will never:

One of the pillars within my personal constitution is to be a great steward in all areas of my life: finances, relationships, resources, and especially my time. Most people don't see time as a resource, but it is. A friend once said, "If you have time, you can make money, and if you have money, you can buy time." The old adage, "time is money," is more accurate today than ever before and should be treasured because it's the one thing we're always losing.

Managing Time

People are busy, so don't waste their time. When facilitating a meeting, I try to keep it to an hour or less. Anything more is unnecessary, and as far as I'm concerned, disrespectful of people's time. Set an agenda and a desired outcome and get out of there. Conference calls should be for discussion; in-person meetings should be reserved for decisions. **Long meetings are a sign of lack of clarity, bad leadership, and no direction.**

Furthermore, how much is your personal time worth? I know this may seem elementary to some, but there are 24 hours in a day. Are you wasting time on nonproductive conversation and unfruitful relationships when you could be investing your time more wisely? How much time do you spend on basic body care, sleeping, eating, friends, family, gym, social time, and work? Survey your life: Are you spending your time wisely? Does your time and productivity complement or conflict with where you're going?

Below is the formula for calculating the value of your time—not simply your work time, but the value of every hour of your day, *personal and professional,* in hopes that you will use your time wisely and maximize every minute, no matter how small.

- 365 days per year x 24 hours a day = 8,760 hours per year
- Annual income/8,760 = your hourly value
- *Ex. $50,000/8,760 = $5.71 per hour (value of your time)*

Calculate your time:

Your Annual Income $_____ / 8,760 hours per year = $_____per hour.

What's the point? If the value of my time is $5.71 per hour, I should be using my time wisely. If my life isn't what and where I want it to be, I should be creating opportunities to make it productive.

Money vs. Access

Sometimes money gives you the means to make substantial purchases, but it doesn't always give you access. Money and access are not the same. In the past, my best opportunities were created by access, not necessarily by what was in my wallet. People make short-term decisions usually motivated by money. However, decisions made for money don't always offer greater access or a better position in the long run. For example, if a business decision may not net a large income but will provide future opportunities for business, then it provides business access. Access-producing decisions have long-term benefits of a *spiritual, family, fiscal* and/or *career* nature that money alone does not.

- SPIRITUAL: Does it benefit me spiritually?
- FAMILY: Does it improve family relationships?
- FISCAL: Is it an asset (not just cash)? Does it bring value?
- CAREER: Will it enhance my career?

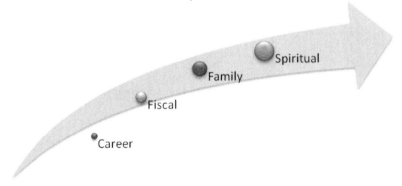

Influence vs. Importance

We live in a culture that thrives on importance and stature, but there is a difference between importance and influence. Importance may bring money and fame, but influence brings change. Influence suggests a personal connection. **People don't ask to be influential. They are influential because other people make them so.** People elevate them because they value what they promote and what they represent. **A person can be important and never be influential.** Saul was important, but David was influential. The Vice President of the United States is important, but Oprah is influential—just ask the beef industry! **A position doesn't automatically earn you respect, but respect gets you influence.**

Influential people engage us in something greater than ourselves.

It's simple: if we can touch the hearts of others, we can reach their treasure and gain influence in their life.

My prayer is that the information in this chapter helps you become the best leader possible. I try as often as I can to serve the people I lead. I must admit that finding the right people and learning how to work well with difficult people isn't always easy, but it's essential for success. Not wasting other people's time is a key leadership quality that will earn you great respect and a reputation for being clear, intentional, and shrewd. The greatest leadership lesson you can ever learn is that seeking access and influence instead of money and importance is the real measure of truly leading with greatness. If only I had known this fifteen years ago!

Chapter Highlights

- Leaders know how to find the right people and to create environments for learning, growth, and self-discovery.

- Most people tend to think leadership is about being on top and guiding others. Actually, leadership is being on the bottom and pushing others to the top.

- A leader's job is to serve his/her team.

- The most dynamic leaders are able to keep the objectives and goals of the project in the forefront, yet support and encourage the team by supplying the team's needs and building on the team's capability and capacity.

- Capability is short-term skills built on past experiences, while capacity builds on future potential.

- Great leaders provide not only intellect, but also inspiration.

- A gifted leader isn't always concerned about what they can get; they value what they can give—of their experience, education, and excellence.

- As a leader, you become indirectly responsible for the emotional development of your team.

- A strong team is one where all members are secure with themselves, their abilities, and the talent they each bring.

- One of the most important leadership skills to develop is working well with all people—difficult, crazy, envious, and insecure.

- In any relationship there are four basic human needs: *acceptance, identity, security,* and *purpose.*

- Man's greatest reward is knowing why he was put on this earth.

- There are only three major decisions we will ever make: our maker, our mission, and our mate.

- What's good for the whole is also beneficial for the individual.

- Disagreements don't have to be destructive or divisive.

- Celebrated leaders recruit good talent, empower them to make strategic decisions, and reprimand employees in such a way that employees see the error of their ways and are motivated to improve.

- Employ some LUV (*Listen, Understand*, and *Validate*) in your communication: Listen to what people say. Understand by repeating what they said. Validate the other person's feelings.

- Importance may bring money and fame, but influence brings change. Influence suggests a personal connection.

- A position doesn't earn you respect, but respect gets you influence.

- Influential people engage us in something greater than ourselves.

- A superb leader is clear and intentional in their communication.

- The greatest leadership lesson you can ever learn is that seeking access and influence instead of money and importance is the real measure of truly leading with greatness.

Up Next ⇨

The final chapter, *Leaving a Legacy of Greatness,* identifies practical legacy tools, including finding a purpose, setting a vision, being open to diversity, creating new experiences, and how to identify the people to whom you will leave your legacy.

Leaving a Legacy of Greatness

CHAPTER 11
Leaving a Legacy of Greatness

Greatness always leaves a legacy. A legacy is anything handed down from the past. It takes courage, vision, and sacrifice to build a legacy of greatness: the courage to do something different, the vision to see the big picture, and the maturity to sacrifice and respect the time needed. Often in our society, we equate legacy with financial gain. Yet, it's quite possible to earn millions and never leave a legacy. A legacy is the mark one leaves on history and in the world. Leaving a positive legacy should be done with intentionality for the sake of the generations to follow.

Look at the great leaders of our time: Thurgood Marshall, the first black Supreme Court Justice of the United States; Mahatma Gandhi, who was a major political and spiritual leader of the Indian independence movement; President Franklin Delano Roosevelt, who provided leadership against Nazi Germany and instituted new opportunities for African-Americans and women; and Dr. Martin Luther King, Jr., a key leader during the Civil Rights Movement. The impact of their greatness left a legacy. The fruit of these leaders, even today, influences every aspect of our society just as our lives will influence those who come behind us.

Our job is to improve and enlarge everything over which we have direct influence and to prepare the path for those who will come behind us. In the very beginning, God gave five guiding principles for life. Genesis 1:28 (KJV) says, "And God blessed them, and God said unto them, Be fruitful, and multiply, and replenish the earth, and subdue it: and have dominion over the fish of the sea, and over the fowl of the air, and over every living thing that moveth upon the earth." In this verse God mandates five things: be fruitful, multiply, replenish, subdue, and have dominion. To be fruitful means to be productive. Multiplication is to increase. To replenish is to fill again or renew or to stock again. Subduing involves taking territories. To have dominion is to have control. These five directives are key components to leaving a legacy. In my own personal life I've witnessed this progression.

My hard work has enabled me to achieve financial stability (to be fruitful). The productivity of my hard work has allowed me to increase my net worth and accumulate greater wealth, building opportunities (multiplication). The principles I learned while working hard I applied consistently over three years to continue to build wealth (to renew). At the conclusion of the three years, I was able to purchase a new home and continue to grow my net worth (to subdue) and eventually achieve additional territories (dominion).

In my personal pursuit of greatness, I've noticed three types of people: *fruit bearers, fruit sellers,* and *fruit eaters.* Fruit bearers are people who are extremely productive. These fruitful achievers are extremely task-driven and focused on the end result. They make everyone around them better and energize them to step up their game. Fruit sellers are people who persuade and convince others. They can be engaging and have the power to take you toward your promise, or to pull you away from your promise if they are a distraction. Fruit eaters are people who consume or devour gradually. They never risk what they have, but cost others everything.

TYPES OF PEOPLE	THEY ARE	CHARACTERISTICS
fruit bearers	people who are extremely productive	• task-driven and focused on the end result • make everyone around them better and energize them to step up their game
fruit sellers	people who persuade and convince others	• can take you toward your promise or pull you away from your promise
fruit eaters	people who consume or devour gradually	• manipulators who never risk what they have

So Why Is Legacy Important?

Legacy is important for life! No other story demonstrates legacy more poignantly than the relationship between Ruth and Naomi. Naomi's ability to lead and guide Ruth was invaluable for the legacy of future generations, even Christ. The relationship between Naomi and Ruth is a model for all. Naomi's instruction to Ruth...

- Provided opportunity. Ruth 1:6-7 (NLT): *Then Naomi heard in Moab that the Lord had blessed his people in Judah by giving them good crops again. So Naomi and her daughters-in-law got ready to leave Moab to return to her homeland. With her two daughters-in-law she set out from the place where she had been living, and they took the road that would lead them back to Judah.*

- Provided for Ruth's best interests. Ruth 1:11-13 (NKJV): *But Naomi replied, "Why should you go on with me? Can I still give birth to other sons who could grow up to be your husbands? No, my daughters, return to your parents' homes, for I am too old to marry again. And even if it were possible, and I were to get married tonight and bear sons, then what? Would you wait for them to grow up and refuse to marry someone else? No, of course not, my daughters! Things are far more bitter for me than for you, because the Lord himself has raised his fist against me."*

- Provided insight and wisdom. Ruth 2:22-23 (NKJ): *And Naomi said to Ruth her daughter-in-law, "It is good, my daughter, that you go out with his young women, and that people do not meet you in any other field." So she stayed close by the young women of Boaz, to glean until the end of barley harvest and wheat harvest; and she dwelt with her mother-in-law.*

- Provided a mature and supportive perspective. Ruth 3:18 (NLT): *Then Naomi said to her, "Just be patient, my daughter, until we hear what happens. The man won't rest until he has settled things today."*

Legacy extends beyond one individual so both the giver and the recipient benefit. The senior, who leaves the legacy, knows their contributions will help the recipient thrive, and the younger or less established one knows provisions are available for their future success. Naomi and Ruth mutually benefited from their relationship.

The Bible contains other examples of legacy-building relationships as well:

- Elijah performed eight miracles, but under Elijah's tutorage Elisha performed sixteen.
- Eli helped Samuel hear God's voice.
- Paul guided Timothy as a young pastor.

Legacy isn't just about *what* you leave behind but *whom* you empower and inspire to carry on what you leave behind. With limited time and resources, we can't help everyone individually, but we can help a few. The collective wisdom of several generations could change, and has changed, nations—even the world!

But as in so many families, finding the right person to leave your legacy to can be a challenge. How do we identify the characteristics of someone worthy to receive a financial legacy? When making a decision about who to help, use Ruth's character as a guide. A worthy recipient of one's legacy...

- Accepts responsibility. Ruth 1:17 (NLT): *[Ruth said,] "Wherever you die, I will die, and there I will be buried. May the Lord punish me severely if I allow anything but death to separate us!"*

- Works with what they have and seizes opportunities. Ruth 2:2 (NLT): *One day Ruth the Moabite said to Naomi, "Let me go out into the harvest fields to pick up the stalks of grain left behind by anyone who is kind enough to let me do it."*

- Has a great work ethic. Ruth 2:3 (NLT): *So Ruth went out to gather grain behind the harvesters.*

- Has a good reputation. Ruth 2:11; 3:11 (NLT): *"Yes, I know," Boaz replied. "But I also know about everything you have done for your mother-in-law since the death of your husband. I have heard how you left your father and mother and your own land to live here among complete strangers."* And later, Boaz tells Ruth: *"Now don't worry about a thing, my daughter. I will do what is necessary, for everyone in town knows you are a virtuous woman."*

- Has a positive and thankful attitude. Ruth 2:10 (NLT): *Ruth fell at his feet and thanked him warmly. "What have I done to deserve such kindness?" she asked. "I am only a foreigner."*

- Is appreciative. Ruth 2:13 (NLT): *"I hope I continue to please you, sir,"* she replied. *"You have comforted me by speaking so kindly to me, even though I am not one of your workers."*

- Listens and follows wise instruction. Ruth 3:5 (NLT): *"I will do everything you say,"* Ruth replied.

- Gets the big picture and is loyal. Ruth 3:10 (NLT): *"The Lord bless you, my daughter!"* Boaz exclaimed. *"You are showing even more family loyalty now than you did before, for you have not gone after a younger man, whether rich or poor."*

- Exercises discretion. Ruth 3:14 (NLT): *So Ruth lay at Boaz's feet until the morning, but she got up before it was light enough for people to recognize each other. For Boaz had said, "No one must know that a woman was here at the threshing floor."*

Building a Legacy of Greatness

A certain mindset is necessary to leave a legacy for the next generation. Capricious behavior doesn't have the stamina for legacy building; focus and intention do. We must know our purpose, have a vision and goals, create new experiences, diversify our surroundings, examine and grow from failures, and discipline our thoughts and words for greatness.

- *Purpose.* Zig Ziglar perhaps said it best: "Don't become a wandering generality. Be a meaningful specific" (*Goals: Setting And Achieving Them On Schedule*, Nightingale-Conant, 2000). It's impossible to discuss greatness without discussing purpose. We should prepare for, pursue, perfect, and perpetuate our purpose. Surveying our skills, abilities, knowledge, understanding, and wisdom is a good way to determine purpose. One's purpose is the *melting pot* of all five.

  o *Skills* are our special abilities.

  o *Ability* is the power to perform.

  o *Knowledge* is information.

  o *Understanding* is comprehension and the application of knowledge.

  o *Wisdom* is all the above guided by common sense.

Take a moment to survey yourself. What do you think is your purpose?

_____

_____

_____

- *Vision and Goals.* Vision is the act or power of anticipating that which is to come. It is what we practice in front of the mirror. Vision answers the question, "What will I be doing twenty years from now?" *and...*

  o How will I accomplish this vision?

  o Whom do I need to know to accomplish this vision?

  o When will I accomplish this vision?

  o What is keeping me from accomplishing this vision today?

  o Why do I want to accomplish this vision?

Write your vision and three steps toward achieving that vision.

Vision statement:

_____

_____

_____

Steps toward achieving it:

1. _____
2. _____
3. _____

- *Create New Experiences.* Meet new people and experience new things. Try cooking classes, learn a new language, or travel to other countries.

Broaden your perspective on life. *What new experience do you plan to try and by when?*

_____

_____

_____

- *Diversity and Integration.* Sad to say, but the most segregated place on Sunday is church. In the United States we have much diversity but little integration. Diversity is external, but integration is internal. Diversity may be forced, but integration is invited. Look at the racial/cultural makeup of your friends and make adjustments. I'm not saying stand at the bus stop with a sign that says *Looking for Native American, African-American, Caucasian, Latino, or Asian friends.* I'm saying, when you meet people, seek common interests, not common color. **Most people want the core things, such as a better life with more opportunities and true happiness; let the internal attributes bind you, not the external.** In twenty years, the world will be more diverse than you can imagine. Don't allow your prejudice to limit your capacity for greatness by limiting the people you know.

How many friends of other races/cultures do you have? How and where can you meet other people who don't look like you?

_____

_____

_____

- *Examine and Grow from Failures.* Failures let us know we are off-focus. They help us revise the plan. Without failures we wouldn't know how we were doing. The adversary wants failures to distract and discourage us, but God wants failures to deliver us and help us grow. Don't let a failure be a monument that demands too much of your attention; make it a motivator.

What failures have become monuments that you need to use instead as motivators?

Monuments:

_____

_____

_____

Motivators:

_____

_____

_____

- *Discipline Your Words and Thoughts.* What we say and think are indicators of where we are. The words we say out of our mouths, our inner thoughts, the stories we tell ourselves—these all become emotions we exhibit. Resist the urge to engage negative words and thoughts. The sooner we begin to filter our words and thoughts and to believe God's Word over our own insecurities, the better our potential for greatness.

Using the graph on the next page, write what words and thoughts keep you from greatness. Then write a new positive script, based on what God says about you.

Current Words/Thoughts	New Script
I'm not smart enough to own my own business.	*God says He has given me gifts and abilities and I can excel beyond what I ever hoped or imagined.*

Finally, to continue the intention of leaving a legacy of greatness, write two letters.

1. Write a letter to yourself about your legacy thus far. What have you accomplished? Whom have you positively influenced?

2. Write a letter to the next generation. What do you want them to know? What lessons have you learned that you want to teach them?

I have a saying: sometimes the period is just the beginning. In writing, the period sets the stage for something that follows: a new sentence, a new paragraph, or a new page. In life, the period concludes our bio but starts someone else's. Legacy concludes our physical life but not our contributions. It's where our contributions are perfected—a head start for future generations. What will you start? How will you be remembered? What will you contribute? What will be your greatness?

Chapter Highlights

- A legacy is more than leaving a monetary inheritance; it's a family's mark in history and on the world.

- Our job is to improve and enlarge everything over which we have direct influence and to prepare the path for those who will come behind us.

- In Genesis 1:28, God mandates five things: that we be fruitful, multiply, replenish, subdue, and have dominion.

- Legacy extends beyond the individual so both the giver and the recipient benefit.

- Legacy isn't just about *what* you leave behind but *whom* you empower and inspire to carry on what you leave behind.

- The collective wisdom of several generations could change, and has changed, nations—even the world!

- Capricious behavior doesn't have the stamina for legacy building; focus and intention do.

- We must know our purpose, have a vision and goals, create new experiences, diversify our surroundings, examine and grow from failures, and discipline our thoughts and words for greatness.

- We should prepare for, pursue, perfect, and perpetuate our purpose.

- Diversity is external, but integration is internal. Diversity may be forced, but integration is invited.

- Failures let us know we are off-focus. They help us revise the plan.

- The adversary wants failures to distract and discourage us, but God wants failures to deliver us and help us grow.

- Don't let a failure be a monument; make it a motivator.

- The sooner we begin to filter our words and thoughts and believe God's Word over our own insecurities, the better our potential for greatness.

Afterword

Congratulations. You now know that greatness can be grasped! As we evolve, our ability to successfully produce is directly enhanced by our inner ability to visualize the outcome. Our lives are more about when and how we transition. Applying the tools in this book will enable you to claim and possess the place you are destined to occupy. Although targeted for young professionals, *Chasing Greatness* has something for all adults. Here's to greatness; now go chase it!

Chasing Greatness is more than a book; it's a movement of individuals dedicated to moving from ordinary lives to extraordinary greatness! We are so committed to improving leadership in the world that we have launched ChasingGreatness.com, a companion online membership community to the *Chasing Greatness* book. The site is dedicated to individuals who really want to pursue greatness with more intentionality. For more information, visit www.ChasingGreatness.com.

About the Author

Towan Isom is a writer, speaker, gifted teacher, and seasoned entrepreneur. *Chasing Greatness: The Young Professional's Guide to a Dynamic Life* is her first book. Towan is the founder of Spiritually Speaking, a ministry that started with ten people and has grown to over 8,000 members. Towan has a successful marketing consulting firm and knows the strategies for living a dynamic life.

Towan was born in Wilson, N.C., and raised in Washington, D.C. Despite humble beginnings, Towan managed to obtain a real estate net worth of $1 million by age 25 and to start a successful marketing firm at age 27. Drawing from professional and personal experiences, Towan entertains, educates, and encourages audiences with an animated personality and razor-sharp wit.

Towan's message is for all audiences with a desire for greatness. If you value personalized instruction rooted in Godly principles, invite Towan to your next business, church, or conference event. With *CHASING GREATNESS SEMINARS,* Towan has developed eleven 45- to 60-minute sessions based on the chapters in this book to assist your group in discovering their greatness.

Contact Towan Isom
ISOM Media LLC
info@chasinggreatness.com
www.chasinggreatness.com